CELLO STORY

Jean
1934

CELLO STORY

DIMITRY MARKEVITCH

Translated from the French by
Florence W. Seder

Summy-Birchard Inc.

Alfred Music
P.O. Box 10003
Van Nuys, CA 91410-0003
alfred.com

ISBN-10: 0-87487-406-8
ISBN-13: 978-0-87487-406-8

Contents

About the Author

FOR CONCERT CELLIST DIMITRY MARKEVITCH, authenticity is of paramount importance. A close disciple of the late Gregor Piatigorsky, he begins his preparation of any work with an intensive study of the score—preferably the original manuscript. During such research, he rediscovered a set of manuscripts of Bach's suites for unaccompanied cello, which he edited for publication in the United States by Theodore Presser. Markevitch introduced the new edition at a memorable concert in Carnegie Hall. He has also rediscovered a lost sonata for cello and piano, opus 64 of Beethoven, which he edited for publication by Presser. He has contributed to editions of works by Mussorgsky, de Falla, Stravinsky, and Shostakovitch.

Another manifestation of Markevitch's concern for authenticity is his use of a baroque cello in performing music that predates the nineteenth century. His instrument—made at the beginning of the eighteenth century by Jacques Bocquay, one of the first great French luthiers—has been carefully restored by Étienne Vatelot of Paris, a master instrument maker, and Luthfi Becker, a specialist in baroque instruments. Markevitch plays this instrument with an authentic baroque bow—a copy made for him by Jean-Yves Matter of Strasbourg of a bow contemporary with his cello that is now in the Museum of Instruments of the Paris Conservatory. The French film director François Reichenbach has made a film in which Markevitch demonstrates the differences between a modern cello and a baroque.

Dimitry Markevitch made the first complete recording of the Sonata for unaccompanied cello opus 8 of Zoltan Kodály. He has also recorded the Sonata for cello and piano opus 40 of Shostakovitch and two sonatas for cello and piano by Louis Abbiate (with Bernard Ringeissen). He is a member of the American Musicological Society and of the Société Française de Musicologie; and he founded the Institute for Advanced Musical Studies in Switzerland. He teaches cello at the École Normale de Musique and at the Conservatoire Serge Rachmaninoff—both in Paris.

Prelude

WHEN YOU ASK A MUSIC LOVER to name his favorite instrument, there is a strong likelihood he will answer: "The cello—no other instrument possesses to such a degree the tones of the human voice nor touches the heart so directly." However, a humorist might say: "The cello? It is simply a double bass that has had bad luck."

For nearly five hundred years, the development of the cello has traveled a rocky road, full of ups and downs. I am going to try—to the best of my ability—to describe its history, which is truly an epic. This endeavor will be a labor of love, for the cello has become a large part of my life, and I have known it for a long time. Each day, I succeed in uncovering more of its resources, which are virtually inexhaustible. The possibilities for musical expression which it alone offers are immense. With it, one can appreciate Verlaine's vow: "music, above all things." It is my friend . . . my confidant; and everything that concerns it interests me.

The cello is fascinating in all its aspects: its origin, its development, its great makers, its celebrated players, the music written for it, the mysteries of its superb sonority—and a great many others. These aspects taken individually might each serve as the basis of a separate work. Publications dealing primarily with the cello are limited, however, and most of them dwell on the mistaken concept that the cello is a derivative of the gamba—an error based on false premises but the general rule for many years. Unfortunately, this myth that the viola da gamba was the ancestor of the cello is still well established in certain minds. I hope the section devoted to the origin and history of the instrument presented here sheds some light on this problem.

The great performing artists of the cello have been the object of veritable worship on the part of their admirers, for this beautiful instrument never fails to stir the emotions; and those adept at playing it have a vehicle that enables them to display—and evoke—great passion.

Thus history, fact, and personal anecdote blend here to provide a complete story of the instrument. May this book entertain you, help you to know the cello to the fullest, and lead you to love it as I do.

CELLO STORY

Figure 1. Luthier Luthfi Becker at his workbench assembling the body of a cello.

The Instrument

MAKING STRINGED INSTRUMENTS (*lutherie*) is a noble profession. What a marvelous vocation—to know how to choose woods, to handle them, and to fashion them into works of art that come to life in the hands of artists interpreting the music of the great composers.

Watching an instrument-maker of today closely, one sees him follow the same procedures his illustrious predecessors used four hundred years ago (*Figure 1*). Andrea Amati (c. 1505–c. 1580)—the first great maker from Cremona, the Italian center of lutherie—constructed a cello in the same way it is done today. He needed about fifty pieces of specific kinds of wood, which he had to cut to a particular design, then model, sculpt, assemble, stain, and varnish—all by hand. One cannot escape being fascinated by the results—these thrilling members of the violin family. They allow one to express the most profound feelings, to convey emotions that stir the soul, and yet to give a sensation of total peace.

Let us carefully examine a violoncello in an attempt to penetrate the mystery of this miraculous object (*Figure 2*). The woods are rather ordinary: Swiss or Tyrolean pine for the top, maple for the back, sides, neck, and scroll (as well as the bridge), and ebony for the fingerboard, tailpiece, and pegs. (These last three were originally made of boxwood or maple.) If the shape of the body, whose principal function is to amplify the vibration of the strings, were less elaborate, there would be a risk of favoring some notes at the expense of others. For this reason, after centuries of trial and error, this method of reducing acoustical interference and minimizing distortion was finally reached. This was achieved by curving the reflecting surfaces to varying degrees. Further attempts to improve the existing model have been totally fruitless.

DESCRIPTION AND NOMENCLATURE

At first glance, the cello seems to be very simple: just a body (the sounding box), the neck, four strings, and various small fittings. Its construction, however, demands extreme care and great precision. From the standpoint of both acoustics and esthetics, the choice of materials is extremely important; and the assembly of the different parts, the matching and joining of the grain of the wood must be meticulously done.

The *top* (1), which is the sounding board, consists of two pieces of pine glued together. It is the most important element in determining the quality of the tone. Its thickness increases from about 3.6 mm at the edges to 4.8 mm at the center. This top is pierced by two holes shaped in the form of an ***f*** (2), whose function is to allow the air, and consequently the sound waves, to flow freely from the interior of the body.

The *back* (3) is usually made of maple, although there are some examples in poplar. It can be a single piece of wood, but it is more frequently constructed of two, glued together, and it is slightly thicker than the top. Shaping the top and back and determining their thickness are done—more or less depending on the maker or the time—through the delicate use of a plane. Both shape and thickness are minutely measured with calipers.

The *sides* (4), sometimes called the ribs or shoulders, consist of six thin bands of maple that have been shaped over a hot iron mold to conform to the outline of the top and back, which they hold together.

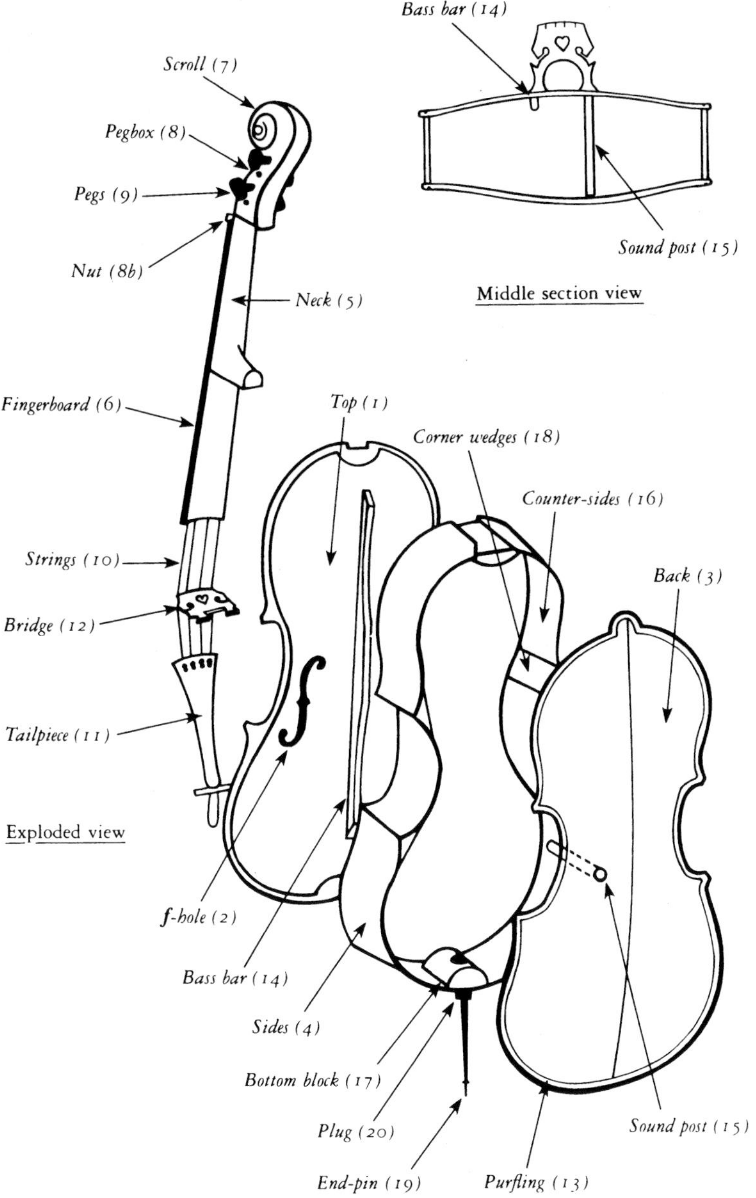

Figure 2. The nomenclature of the cello.

The *neck* (5), also made of maple, supports the *fingerboard* (6) which is made of ebony and is topped by the *scroll* (7) and the *peg box* (8). Between the base of the peg box and the top of the fingerboard is the *nut* (8b), a small piece of ebony (ivory on the earliest cellos) whose function is to give the strings their proper height above the fingerboard and keep them correctly spaced from one another by means of four grooves. The peg box holds the *pegs* (9), devices, to which the upper ends of the *strings* (10) are attached, the lower ends being fastened to an ebony *tailpiece* (11) at the bottom of the cello. In between, the strings pass over the *bridge* (12), which is made of maple and can be found between the two ***f**-holes*. This bridge is of prime importance because it is the means of transmitting the vibrations of the strings to the top of the cello. Delicately cut, it is only a few millimeters thick at the bottom—and it gradually thins out toward the top. It is not glued in place but held upright solely by the pressure of the strings, which has been found to be around 100 pounds. The exact placement (or *setting*) of the bridge demands the utmost skill on the part of the maker.

The *purfling* (13) consists of extremely thin strips of wood, generally three in number—two black with a lighter-colored one between them—inlaid along the outside edges of the top and back. They are purely decorative, but they are widely thought to help prevent the wood from cracking.

In the interior we find the following:

The *bass bar* (14) is a rib of pine glued to the under side of the top and lying lengthwise under the left foot of the bridge. Its role is twofold: to reinforce the top by supporting the pressure of the strings and to enhance the sonority of the bass notes.

The *sound post* (15) is a small, cylindrical pole of pine, wedged (not glued) between the back and the top slightly below the right foot of the bridge. Its purpose is to transfer the vibrations from the top to the back, thus strengthening the tone. To achieve the latter, it must be placed precisely at the point where the vibrations form a focal point.

The *counter-sides* (16) are strips of wood that evenly line the sides.

The *top and bottom blocks* (17) and the *corner wedges* (18) are small blocks of wood glued to the inner surface to give solidity to the entire structure.

The *end-pin* (19), also called the tail-pin, is an ebony or metal post that is part of the *tail-button or plug* (20), the socket at the bottom of the cello to which the tailpiece is attached. The end-pin extends into the body through the tail-button. Its length can be adjusted by moving it in or out, and it is held in position by tightening a screw. Although virtually indispensable now, the pin is a fairly new addition. In recent years, some players have been experimenting with bent end-pins. These give the instrument a more horizontal position—one preferred by certain artists.

The overall length of a cello is approximately 130 cm, its body length is 76 cm, and its depth from top to back is 11 cm toward the neck, increasing to 12 cm toward the tailpiece.

Although the design appears to be symmetrical, we can see that the cello is wholly asymmetrical in its interior. The sound-post is to the right and the bass bar to the left, in order to obtain the greatest possible intensity of resonance. Consequently, the tones produced by a pushed bow (up-bow) are more favored than those produced by a pulled bow (down-bow).

Let me conclude this description with a few words about varnish, a subject of passionate controversy for generations. Once an instrument is assembled, but before its accessories are added, it is covered with several coats of varnish. It is generally thought that varnish contributes more to the appearance than to the sound, but it is also conceded that bad varnish certainly deadens the tone. Varnishes with oil, benzine, or alcohol bases are used, each maker having his own 'recipe', but I do not think the secret lies in the ingredients so much as in the knack of applying them, although the varnish used by the celebrated old Italian makers contained oil that dried very slowly.

No cello has a voice without its *strings*, four in number, which were originally made from catgut and later from sheep gut. Jean de Laborde in his "Essai sur la musique ancienne et moderne," of 1780, considered those of Naples "clear, transparent, without knots . . . properly proportioned to each other so that they produce perfect fifths and octaves, on which everything will depend."

Very early, strings of steel or brass were tried, but some gambists were the only ones to favor them. From the eighteenth century on, the two lower strings were of gut covered with brass or silver wire.

Recently, the use of steel strings has become widespread because of their durability and greater volume but at a loss of tone quality. Strings made of nylon, and especially of perlon, have also been tried with success.

The *mute* is a small accessory made of ebony, metal, or leather, which—when fastened to the top of the bridge—lessens the vibrations and thus modifies the tone quality and produces special effects. Known since the beginning of the seventeenth century, it was used by Lully and was highly valued by the Impressionist composers.

ORIGIN AND HISTORY

Tracing the origin of the violoncello is an extremely complicated task because of several factors, of which the principal ones are these:

1. Authentic and reliable sources are scarce. Some of the most interesting having been destroyed by fire, flood, pillage, vandalism, vermin, wars, or other disasters. Inestimably important documents disappeared during the course of World War II.
2. An extremely small number of instrumental specimens survives from the period prior to 1550. Large-scale models in particular suffered from the ravages of time because their size made them vulnerable, and others were transformed or altered by unscrupulous makers, an unfortunate custom that has led to the disappearance of invaluable specimens.
3. Certain texts are available only in translation and because these are often unfaithful, there is much confusion. For example, the German word *Geige* becomes *gigue* in French. Then we have *vielle* becoming *viola*, later to be translated as *viole* or *fiddle*—although these terms frequently refer to totally different instruments.
4. Diverse books of reference, encyclopedias, dictionaries, and musical histories often do nothing but return to earlier texts, quoting paragraphs from them—even entire chapters—thus perpetuating the same errors.

Consequently, in lieu of an exhaustive study of this exciting subject, I here present a synthesis of my personal studies and of the most serious research of the present time.

It is evident that stringed instruments played by the application of a bow originated in very remote times. The first of them made their appearance in India and in the Far East. Depending on the time of their importation into Europe, their migration probably followed the paths of Arab tribes, Gypsies, and nomadic Jews.

These instruments can be classified in two important categories—the *rebec* family and the *vielle* family. The rebec, pear-shaped and arched at the bottom, generally had three strings tuned in fifths and no frets. (*Frets*, occasionally called *nuts* because of their relationship to the nut at the base of the peg box, were thin strips of catgut placed at regular intervals on the neck or fingerboard to mark off the halftones.) The *lyra*, an antecedent of the rebec and apparently of the same family, had several strings and was vaguely reminiscent of the ancient lyre. It had a rectangular body, rounded at the corners and pierced by

Figure 3. This thirteenth-century musician is playing, cello fashion, a three-stringed instrument (with four pegs—and apparently unfretted). From Cantigas de Santa Maria of the Codex of Alfonso X, the Learned (1221–1284), king of Castile and Leon. *Courtesy Biblioteca y archivo de musica, Real Monasterio de San Lorenzo del Escorial, Spain.*

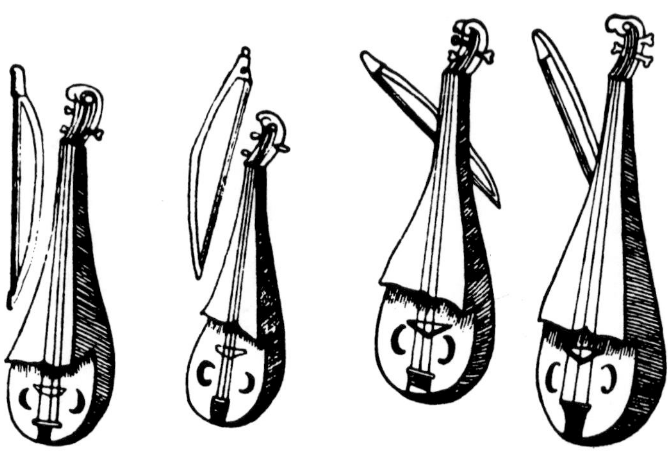

Figure 4. A quartet of unfretted, three-stringed *Polnische Kleingeigen*. From Martin Agricola's *Musica Instrumentalis Deudsch* (1529). Agricola's real name was Martin Sore (1486–1556).

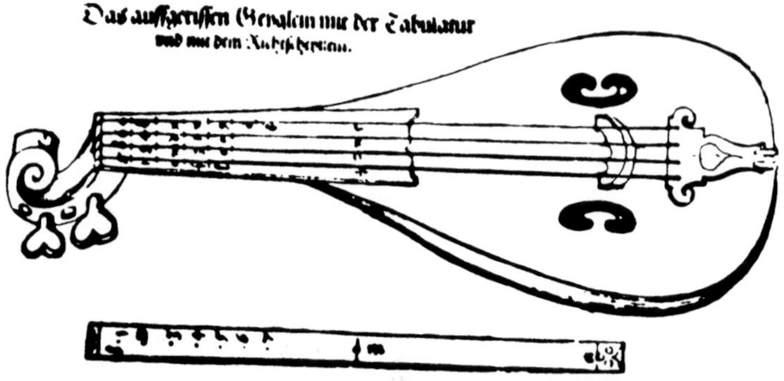

Figure 5. According to Hans Gerle in 1532, the bass member of the *Geygen*, obviously derived from the rebec, was tuned like the modern cello.

two sounding holes. The *rābāb*, of Arabian origin, was very similar to the rebec.

Instruments comparable to these can be found from the twelfth century to the sixteenth century (*Figure 3*). The German author Martin Agricola, describing their tuning in his *Musica Instrumentalis*, speaks of a family of four instruments called *Polnische Geigen* (*Figure 4*). From this time on, most of the instruments appeared in a family grouping, in which each member corresponded to a different range of the human voice, soprano, alto, tenor, and bass, although certain groups comprised as many as six distinct members. In 1532, Hans Gerle, of the renowned Nuremberg family of makers, published *Musica Teusch auf Instrument der Grossen und Kleinen Geygen* in which he described the "*Kleinen Geygen*," which was derived from the rebec but in whose family the bass was tuned like a modern cello (*Figure 5*).

As early as the end of the fifteenth century, another instrument tuned in fifths appeared in Italy. Called *lira da braccio* it was widely portrayed by the painters of the Renaissance. It foreshadowed the violin family even more clearly, especially in the sound-holes, which by then had acquired an ***f***-shape instead of the former ***c***-shape, and in its lack of frets. There was also a complement to the bass, the *lira da gamba* (*Figure 6*)—so named because it was held between the legs (whereas the lira da braccio was held in the arms). Most of these instruments had a brilliant, even shrill, tone perfectly suited to the popular outdoor celebrations, dances, and balls where they were used. In fact, some police ordinances even tried to confine them to taverns and cabarets. It seems that the ancestors of the violin family had a poor beginning.

In contrast, the *vielles* (often called *fiddles* in English) were played by both professionals and distinguished amateurs and were regarded much more highly (*Figure 7*). The large number of study manuals published in the sixteenth century attests to the popularity of these instruments in cultivated circles. Because the configuration was not established definitely for many centuries, it was mandatory that the authors of these manuals describe the instruments and include illustrations in order to avoid all misunderstanding.

In a treatise entitled *Tractatus de Musica* from the end of the thirteenth century, Hieronymous de Moravia left us the first description of the technique of bowed instruments, particularly of the rebec and the vielle (not to be confused with the *vielle à roue*, a hurdy-gurdy of the Auvergne peasants). This vielle had an oval body, a flat top and back connected by sides, and a neck that soon appeared with frets. The number of strings varied at first, and they were usually tuned in fourths. The *rote* was a large vielle used for bass parts. The body shape of these vielles changed according to the inclination and experimentation of the makers. The influence of other factors, such as time and place, as well as the influence of the Spanish *vihuela da arco*, was evident.

Only at the end of the sixteenth century did this family of instruments—by then called *violas da gamba* because they were played in an upright position and cradled between the calves of the legs—arrive at its definitive form (*Figure 8*). At that time, they could be found in several sizes: soprano, alto, tenor, bass, and contra-bass, which collectively became the *viols* of the eighteenth century. For some time, the number of strings varied between three and seven, finally becoming established at six (although the French favored the seven-stringed bass viol). Viols were tuned in fourths, except for the interval between the third and fourth strings, which was a major third. Because this tuning resembled that of the lute, lutenists, of whom there were many, could easily switch from one instrument to the other.

Viols first became popular in Italy; and during the sixteenth and seventeenth centuries, their popularity spread to other countries, especially Germany. In France, their age of glory came during the reign of Louis XIV with the flourishing of such artists as Antoine Forqueray, Caix d'Hervelois, Jean Rousseau, and Marin Marais (1656–1728)—the greatest of them all. Eventually their popularity began to wane. In 1740, Hubert le Blanc, a doctor of law, tried in vain to stem the disappearance of his favorite instrument by publishing "Defense of the bass viol against . . . the pretensions of the violoncello." In England, the viol survived until the death of Carl Friedrich Abel (1725–1787), its major exponent. The most beautiful surviving viols are the work of Joachim Thielke (1641–1719) of Hamburg.

The viol was associated almost exclusively with the aristocracy, for whom it was played *in consort* (by small ensembles) to enhance the

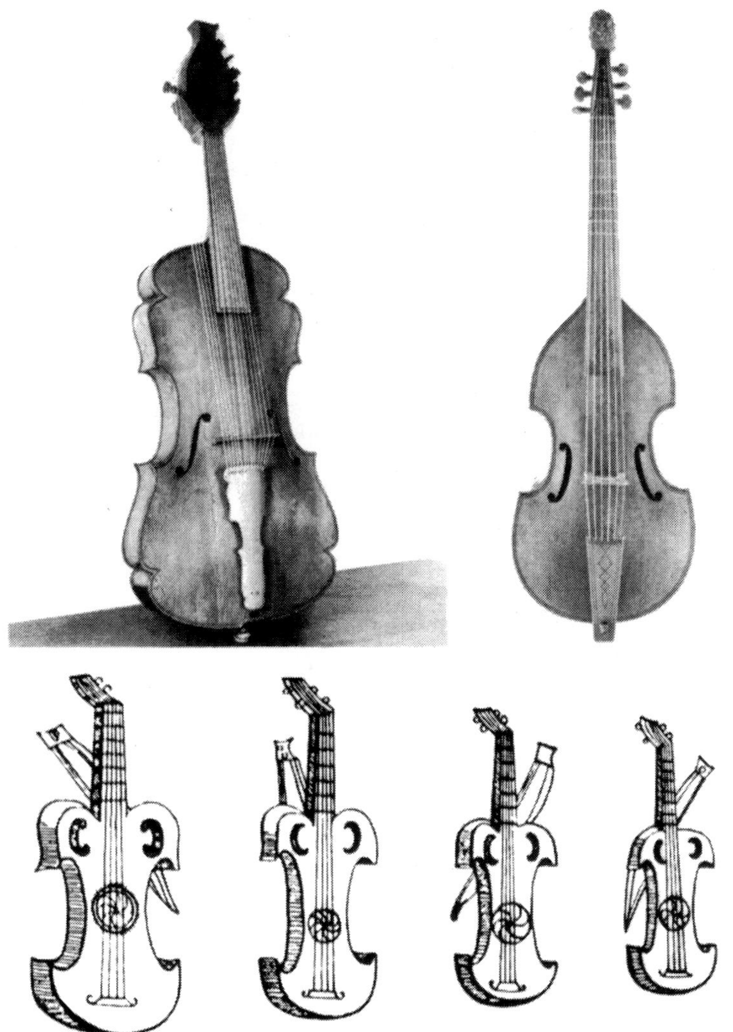

Figure 6 (top left). A lira da gamba by Wendelin Tieffenbrucker, c. 1590. This instrument has thirteen strings; the four alongside the fingerboard are *bourdons*, or drones, for low sustained tones. *Courtesy Kunsthistorisches Museum, Vienna.*

Figure 7 (bottom). The fiddle, called *Grossgeigen* by Agricola. Notice the frets and the features of the lute.

Figure 8 (top right). A small bass (lyra) viol by John Rose, London, 1598—a typical example of the work of this great English maker. *Courtesy Hill Collection, Ashmolean Museum, Oxford.*

Figure 9. Details of a painting, c. 1581, attributed to Jacques Patin, showing a ball at the Valois court. The group of violins (a quartet) includes a rather large cello. A similar painting at Penhurst Place, Kent, shows a smaller cello. *Courtesy Musée des Beaux-Arts de Rennes.*

pleasure of their leisure hours. Philibert Jambe de Fer (1525–1572), a musician from Lyon, in *Epitome Musical* (1556) declared: "We give the name 'viols' to those instruments with which gentlemen, merchants and other people of virtue spend their time. We call the other kind 'violins' and they are used in community dancing—for good reason: they are easier to tune, since a fifth is more pleasant to the ear than a fourth. They are also easier to carry, which is most necessary when playing for weddings or mummery" (*Figure* 9).

Besides the violin itself, the group called *violins* contained the alto (or viola), the tenor (which fell into disuse during the eighteenth century), and the violoncello, which had acquired its configuration by 1500. The first known representation of this instrument is found in a fresco painted by Gaudenzio Ferrari in 1535, which shows an unmistakable cello being played by an angel (*Figure 10*). At that time the instrument was called the *bassa di viola da braccio*, the name of the violin family having formerly been *viola da braccio*. The word *vyollon* had already appeared by 1523 in the records of the court of Savoy, and *violino* was used in 1538 on the occasion of a visit by Pope Paul III to the peace conference in Nice, to which he took his "violini Milanesi" to impress Francis I and Charles V.

The first use of the word *violoncello*, however, did not occur until 1665, when it appeared on "Sonata for 2 or 3, with an optional part

Figure 10. Detail of a fresco painted 1535–1536 by Gaudenzio Ferrari showing a choir of angels. The angel playing a primitive type of cello (notice that the *f*-holes are reversed) is our best proof of the emergence of the cello before 1535. The painting, which is in the cupola of the Cathedral of Saronno, Italy (about fifteen miles north of Milan), also shows a violin and a viola.

Figure 11 (left). A basse de violon and its bow. From *Harmonie Universelle* (Paris, 1636) by Marin Mersenne (1588–1648).

Figure 12 (right). The bas-geig de braccio, a large five-stringed instrument. Probably because of its size, it is fitted with an end-pin. From *Syntagma musicum* (Wolfenbüttel, 1620) by Michael Praetorius.

for the violoncello" which Guido Arresti published in Venice. Meanwhile, it was called *basse de violon* (*Figure 11*), *bassus*, *französische bass*, *bas-geig* (*Figure 12*), *viola de basso*, *violone*, *viulunzeel*, *violoncino* (*Figure 13*), and a multitude of other names. The word *violoncello* did not appear in France until the beginning of the eighteenth century. At that time, it actually referred to two groups of instruments of similar form but different size:

Da chiesa designated the larger size. These were used for church (chiesa) music (the clergy being the biggest customers of the luthiers) and in processions. In regard to this use, Jambe de Fer notes: "Because of its weight, the bas was very difficult to carry, so it was held up by means of a strap attached to a hook in a loop of iron—or some other material—which was fastened to the back of the instru-

Figure 13 (left). Painting of a violoncino by Peter Claez, 1623. A small five-stringed example of the Brescia school. Note the extremely short fingerboard. *Courtesy Musée de Louvre, Paris.*

Figure 14 (right). This drawing by the Dutch artist Leonard Bramer (1596–1674) shows a five-stringed basse de violon carried suspended by a strap.

ment in such a way that it did not interfere with the playing" (*Figure 14*).

Da camera designated the smaller size. These were comparable to the cellos of today, and they met the need felt at the end of the seventeenth century for a concert instrument that could be developed into a solo instrument.

In 1752, J. J. Quantz advised, "The player who not only accompanies with the cello but also plays solos, would do well to have two instruments, one for solo work and another for playing in large musical groups. For the latter use it is necessary that the instrument be larger and its strings be heavier than those on the smaller model. If one were to use a small, lightly strung instrument for both functions, the accompaniment would have no effect in a large musical group. The bow used to accompany must also be stronger, and have black hair, because this activates the strings more strongly than the white."[1]

The difference between the two sizes was not great, the body of the larger measuring between 77 cm and 85 cm and that of the smaller as much as 76 cm. Very few violoncelli da chiesa survive, however, because most of them were cut down to make smaller models.

There were generally four strings, tuned in the following manner:[2]

The tuning of the *violoncello da chiesa* was the most logical, because it allowed the entire violin family to tune together to the same open string, the G, and to cover a continuous expanding range:

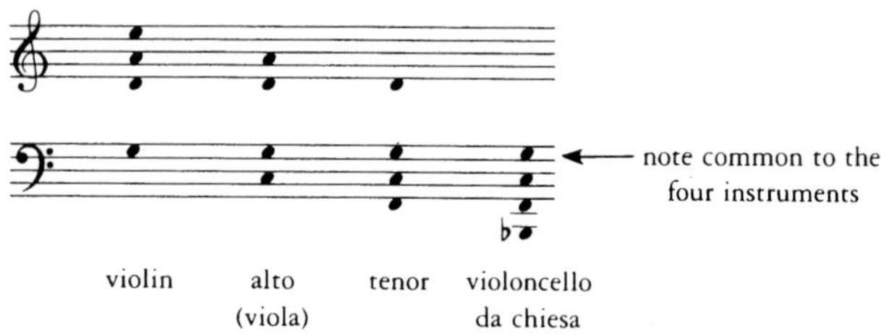

With the *violoncello da camera*, which no longer had the heavy strings necessary for low notes, the tuning was raised one whole step to this:

which became the standard tuning of today's cellos. For a time, the following tuning was also widely used:

1. J. J. Quantz, *Versuch einer Anweisung die Flöte traversiere zu spielen* (Berlin, 1752). Quantz, who discusses considerably more than the flute, is one of our best sources about baroque performance practice.

2. According to Silvestro Ganassi, in *Lettione seconda* (Venice, 1543), Chapter 23, there were only three strings during the first part of the sixteenth century, tuned as follows:

This tuning retained the advantage of having the G common with the other instruments. Occasionally, five-string tuning was also found (*Figure 15*):

and, very exceptionally, six:

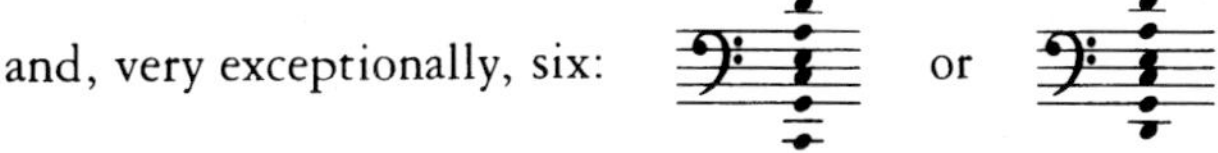

It should be remembered that these tunings were relative. The standard pitch of A was not established until 1859, when it was set at 435 vibrations per second. In 1939, it was raised to 440. Before 1859, instrumentalists tuned to the pitch of an organ, if one was available, which could vary enormously from one organ to another. Otherwise, one followed the rather surprising advice of Hans Gerle in 1527: "To tune, make the string as tight [high in pitch] as possible, without breaking it."

By the second quarter of the eighteenth century the violoncello da camera had been almost universally adopted; and one might say that the modern cello had been born. Significant changes were nevertheless made at the beginning of the nineteenth century, probably through the influence of such violinists as Giovanni Battista Viotti (1753–1824) and Ludwig Spohr (1784–1859), who sought not only ways to be heard to better advantage in larger concert halls and before larger audiences but also a greater ease of technical execution—especially for the high notes of virtuoso passages. Working toward the same objective, the Mantegazza brothers of Milan quickly imitated some of the French luthiers—such as François Pique (1758–1822), Nicholas Lupot (1758–1824), and Jean-Gabriel Koliker (c.1760–1820). Working in the "French mode," they conceived many changes, which they regarded as improvements, for all members of the violin family. They extended the neck and tilted it toward the back, thereby obtaining a greater angle with the bridge, which they had heightened (*Figure 16*). These changes created greater tension in the strings, which in turn increased the weight and pressure on the top by about 35 pounds. Accordingly, the bass bar was strengthened and elongated to provide more support, and the sound-post was made stronger. The

Figure 15. Painting of a cello player by the Flemish artist Dirk Hals (1591–1656). The musician is singing while accompanying himself on a five-stringed cello set on the floor. *Courtesy Wallraf-Richartz Museum, Cologne.*

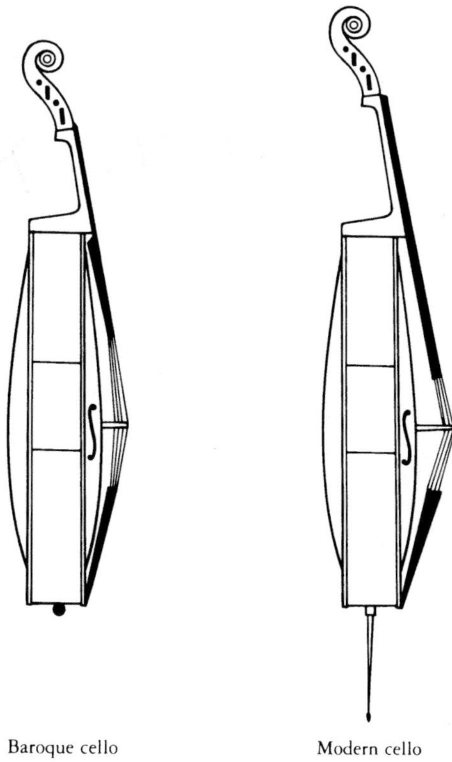

Figure 16. Diagram showing the differences between a baroque cello and a modern one.

resulting instrument was louder and more brilliant in tone and easier to play; but it has never been proven that these changes did not entail the sacrifice of a certain quality of sound. Because instruments are practically impossible to find in their original state, one rarely has the opportunity to make this fascinating comparison for oneself.

For some time, I have been performing baroque music on a cello made about 1700 by Jacques Bocquay, one of the first great French luthiers. It has been restored to its original state by Étienne Vatelot of Paris and by the specialist Luthfi Becker (*Figure 17*).

Figure 17. The author playing his baroque cello, a beautiful example, made about 1700, by the French maker Jacques Bocquay (c. 1680–1730). The bow is a modern replica of a bow of the same period now in the Madame de Chambure collection at the Musée Instrumental du Conservatoire National, Paris. *Photograph by Jean-François Delon.*

THE BOW

The bow is an essential element whose importance is often underestimated (*Figure 18*). Actually, the choice of a bow is as important as that of an instrument—in the course of one concert, the total movement of a bow can cover nearly a mile. The length and weight, the choice of wood and its flexibility, the quality of the hair and of the rosin that coats it are among the prime factors that greatly influence the tone and technical precision of a bow.

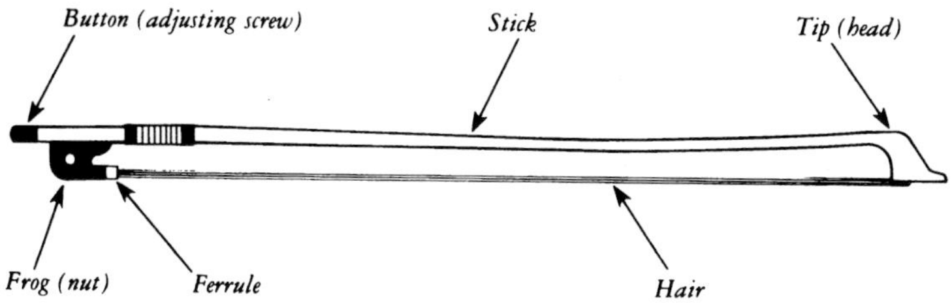

Figure 18. The nomenclature of the bow.

The bow has three essential parts: the *stick*, the *frog*, and the *hair*. The stick is usually cut from an exotic wood called *pernambuca*, which is bent by exposure to heat. (Snakewood was used for older bows.) The frog or nut, made of ebony and decorated with mother-of-pearl, holds the hair under tension that can be regulated by means of a screw or *button* in the end of the stick.

The hair is taken from the tails of horses, the best coming from Siberia. About two hundred strands are needed for each bow, and they should be replaced once or twice a year, depending on the amount of use the bow receives. These strands must be rubbed repeatedly with rosin—a product made by mixing the residue of pine resin with turpentine—to produce a coating that makes the hair sticky enough to cling to the strings as it is drawn across them. The resulting friction causes the strings to vibrate. Rosin is made up into small, round, flat cakes, and it has apparently been in use for a long time:

Hans Gerle mentions in his 1532 instruction book for the lute and viol that "it can be procured in an apothecary shop."

The weight of a modern bow may vary from 70 g to 85 g, but the length has been set at about 72 cm for more than a century and a half. Before that time, the general belief was that expressed by theorist Marin Mersenne in *L'Harmonie Universalle* of 1636: "It is of little importance if a bow is longer or shorter, as long as it is the correct length to excite the strings in the way necessary to draw forth a musical sound."

The bow, which probably began as an adaptation of the hunting bow, originated in the Orient. Its slow evolution peaked at the beginning of the nineteenth century, but its history is even more obscure than that of the stringed instruments themselves. Throughout the Middle Ages it remained very convex, as can be seen in certain engravings (*see Figure 3*). Then it gradually became flatter and more tapered; and by the seventeenth and eighteenth centuries, it had become practically straight (*see Figure 11*). For a long time, the frog was stationary, and the tension of the hair was regulated by the pressure of the right thumb. Other systems were devised for achieving this purpose, including toothed frogs. Finally, at the end of the seventeenth century, a primitive version of the system in use today made its appearance.

During the eighteenth century, the design of the bow underwent important changes: from being lightly convex, it became concave; but this process was not systematic. Bows of all shapes, sizes, and weights were tried; and frog designs in particular varied enormously. Less hair was used, which made the ribbon smaller and thinner. After 1750, the stick became longer; so long, in fact, that Jean-Louis Duport, in an essay of 1805, was led to note, "As to those which are of a disproportionate length, I cannot help but find them ridiculous."

Although they were frequently the same, the names of the great bow makers were not as well known as those of the luthiers. In fact, stubborn tradition for anonymity has prevailed among the great bow makers to this day. A few isolated eighteenth-century bows were dated but not signed, and some nineteenth-century bows were imprinted with the names of their makers, but this custom was not general. A few rare and beautiful bows attributed to Stradivari or

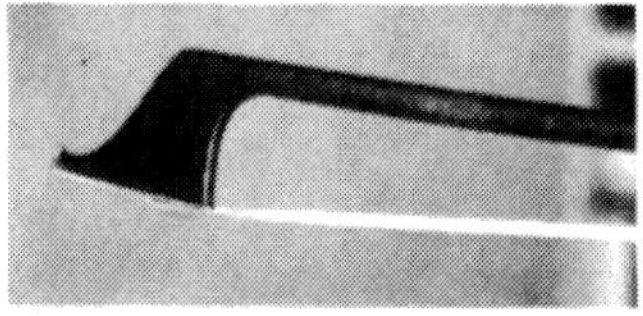
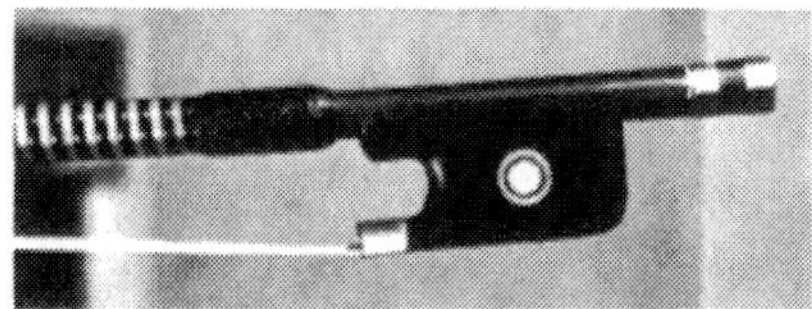

Figure 19. A beautiful example of a cello bow by François Tourte (1747–1835), the "Stradivari of the bow." Made between 1800 and 1810, it is of light brown pernambuca wood with a silver-mounted ebony frog. *Courtesy Janos Scholz collection, New York.*

Montagnana are still in existence; but because of their fragility, very few other specimens have survived. The handful of models that serve us for reference are known by the names of the artists who used them (Corelli, Tartini, Cramer) rather than the names of the makers who fashioned them.

In England, the luthier and bow maker Peter Walmsley flourished in the 1730s. John Dodd (1752–1839), greatest of the English bow makers, used many of the fundamental modifications introduced in France by the Tourtes, father and son. It was the younger, François Tourte (1747–1835) who became the most celebrated of all bow makers. He has been called the "Stradivari of the bow"; and it was he who finally established a design that has not yet been improved (*Figure 19*).

Tourte's bows are neither signed nor dated, but one can recognize and admire them for their beauty of workmanship and purity of line. He used only the best of materials—mostly pernambuco and ebony—with ivory, tortoise shell, mother-of-pearl, gold, and silver. Today, when they can be obtained at all, these masterpieces command remarkably high prices.

By this time, the stick no longer ended in a point, but in a head shaped like a tiny hatchet. The frog (sometimes called the heel) took its definitive form; and a small metal plate or *ferrule* was placed over it where the hair emerged to spread the strands and distribute them more evenly and to hold the hair ribbon flat on the frog.

Tourte used heat to bend the stick to a perfect concave camber and progressively taper it. Although he arrived at this design in a purely empirical way, its success was later shown to be mathematically exact.

In Tourte's bows, the point of equilibrium moved closer to the middle. They were ideal for their resistance, for their lightness, for their resiliency (which responded to the slightest wishes of the artist), and for the uniformity of their tension—whether one played in the middle or at either end. This had not been possible with convex bows.

The difference between the two types of bow embodies a principle of physics, as shown in *Figure 20*. With a convex bow, the hair has a tendency to yield under the pressure exerted by the player—a condition that tends to diminish the sound. At the same time, the resistance of the stick will vary depending upon whether one is playing in the middle or at the ends. The opposite result is produced with a concave bow. One can enlarge and sustain the tone and play with intensity. The design of the stick and the head makes the bow work like a lever, so that there is an almost constant reaction from one end to the other.

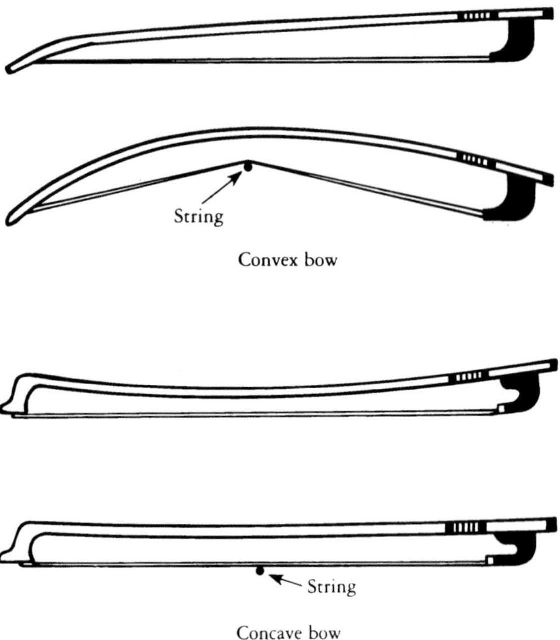

Figure 20. Diagrams of bows, convex and concave.

These improvements to the bow paralleled the modifications made to the instrument around 1800, changes demanded by the artists of the times. Unlike the design of the cello, which had been fixed for a long time, the design of the bow varied considerably before Tourte established a standard. Different types had corresponded to different styles of music. Until about 1750, a short bow was used for French dance music and a long one for Italian sonatas. Until 1725, the French type was the more popular, but thereafter the Italian gradually became the favorite. At the same time, the German bow, which was very short, was supplanted by the French type.

Meanwhile, right-hand technique went through many changes. Its evolution from the early sixteenth century to the present day can be observed in contemporary paintings and methods. In Ferrari's fresco of 1535, the angel playing the cello holds the bow at the frog, with the two middle fingers on top of the stick and the other two and the thumb below (*see Figure 10*). Later, according to Corrette, two basic bow grips developed—the Italian and the French.[3] With the first, the bow was held well up the stick with all the fingers on top and the thumb below. With the second, the first three fingers were on top of the stick, the little finger below, and the thumb under the hair. Corrette also mentions a third bow grip, where the hand is above the frog with the first fingers on top of the stick, the little finger at the extreme end and the thumb under the frog. As late as the beginning of the nineteenth century, a grip in front of the frog, with the little finger barely touching, was recommended by Levasseur and Baudiot.[4] The underhanded bow grip was also used occasionally, especially by converted viola da gamba players.

Although the same bow can sound totally different in the hands of two different players, the older bows possessed certain inherent characteristics: they made it possible to obtain short, clean, unaccented strokes at the heel; chords and crossings from one string to another could be done smoothly; and double stops could be played very clearly—all these practices were perfectly suited to the music of the

3. Michel Corrette, *Méthode théorique et pratique pour apprendre en peu de temps le violoncelle dans sa perfection* (Paris, 1741).

4. Baillot, Levasseur, Catel, et Baudiot, *Méthode de violoncelle adoptée par le Conservatoire Impérial de Musique* (Paris, 1805).

Figure 21. Jean-Baptiste Bréval (1753–1823). Note his playing position and the way he holds the bow beyond the frog. From *Traité du violoncelle* (Paris, 1804).

time. By contrast, the modern Tourte bow, perfectly suited to the musical style of Tourte's time and of later years up to the present, has a marked accentuation and produces a strong, even tone. The expressive, singing character of all romantic music can be obtained only with a bow of this species. Because of these differences, however, it is probably preferable to use an antique bow for music written before 1815. Even at that time, although the Tourte bow was well established, it was not yet universally accepted (*Figure 21*).

Around 1800, Paris was the true center of the development of instrumental technique. This movement was a response to the widening potential afforded by the continuous advancement in the workmanship and perfecting of the French bow, which was brought to a level that has never been surpassed, even though there have been excellent bow makers since.

THE GREAT LUTHIERS

The tremendous vogue for Italian string instruments can be dated precisely to 1827. On a summer day during that year, a tall young man of thirty-five—thin, swarthy, badly shaven, poorly dressed, and covered with dust—strode abruptly into the elegant shop of Jean-François Aldric, the leading Parisian luthier of the day. After some hesitation, the stylish clerk agreed to call his employer. When the latter appeared, the stranger, smiling irresistibly and watching him with deep blue eyes, opened a sack from which he removed first one superb violin and then others—some Guarneris, some Guadagninis, and a magnificent Stradivarius. As he placed them on top of the showcase, he announced in a heavily accented voice, "I am Luigi Tarisio of Milan." Speechless at first, Aldric at length demanded an explanation and learned that all these instruments belonged to the stranger, who had walked from Italy for the express purpose of selling them in this shop.

Born in 1792, Tarisio had resigned himself to becoming a carpenter when a stiffness in the little finger of his left hand put an end to his career as a violinist. A chance encounter with Francesca, the granddaughter of Stradivari, who had become a nun in a convent near Cremona, changed his plans. On the eve of her death, she convinced the young Tarisio that his destiny was not to perform but to perpetuate the name of Stradivari. Since this great maker's death some eighty years earlier, his fame had declined, along with that of the other excellent Italian masters. A great number of their instruments had been abandoned in lofts and cupboards. Although a few artists still played Strads and Guarneris, the fashion had changed; other luthiers, particularly those of the French school of Lupot, had become more highly prized.

Consequently, Tarisio decided to dedicate his life and his energies to searching for—and collecting—all the instruments from the great epoch of Italian violin making that he could uncover. He believed that God had called him to rescue these invaluable masterpieces from ruin and oblivion. He also thought God had endowed him with the ability to recognize them and to unearth them from the unbelievable places where they were hidden. He was often able to obtain instruments he wanted by doing odd jobs of carpentry or by offering new instruments in good condition in exchange. His discoveries had usually lost their strings and needed extensive repairs before they could be played. These old instruments also had to be modified to conform to the style of the day. Once this was done, they became easy to sell, and amateurs bought them up very quickly. Since then, their value has increased steadily; and today, these treasures command astronomical prices.

At that time, only one other person was interested in these old instruments—Count Cozio di Salabue (1755–1840), a nobleman from the Piedmont. Their mutual passion for the old specimens inevitably brought about a meeting between Salabue and Tarisio, and they transacted many business deals. The count sold a number of instruments—among them the celebrated "Messiah" violin. Salabue's collection of more than a hundred instruments included superb specimens by Stradivari, Amati, Guadagnini, and others. After his death, Tarisio bought most of these from the estate.

After his first visit to Paris, this "Knight of Lutherie" returned regularly, always laden with the precious cargo that his unique flair for detection had led him to find all over Italy and elsewhere. His customers, who waited impatiently for him to discover new marvels, were the foremost luthiers of the day—Hart of London; and Thibout, Vuillaume, and Georges Chanot of Paris.

One day, Chanot told Tarisio about a visit he had paid to the shop of a luthier named Ortega in Madrid. There he had acquired a cello top, which Ortega had removed from a Stradivarius. In the course of repairing the instrument, he replaced it with a top of his own making to improve its tone. This was not the first crime of this Spaniard. With incredible vanity and lack of conscience, he had already ruined other beautiful examples, including instruments from the Spanish Court.

Tarisio did not hesitate to set out to find this mistreated cello. He questioned Ortega and—bribing him with 100 francs—learned that the cello belonged to the beautiful Countess Duero. She was not difficult to find; and Tarisio used his Latin charm to persuade her to sell him the disfigured instrument. After prolonged negotiations, they agreed upon a price of 4000 francs; and returning to Paris with the cello, Tarisio asked Vuillaume to replace the original top, which he had already bought from Chanot. This superb instrument, dated 1713, has since been named "The Spanish Bass." Its story is only one example of what this extraordinary individual—Luigi Tarisio—did for the fame and survival of the great Italian instruments. Hundreds of instruments passed through his hands, but few people know that it was by his grace that they were salvaged for us. He made his correspondents promise that these marvels would be entrusted only to young, deserving artists. Although this condition was not always respected, great performers have had instruments worthy of their talents at their disposal for 150 years.

When Tarisio died in 1854, his heirs found 144 magnificent instruments in the miserable attic in Milan where he had lived. Vuillaume bought the lot for 79,150 francs; and eventually he sold all but one of them for more than 1,000,000. The one he kept for himself throughout his life is the violin called the "Messiah," which has never been played and is considered the most perfect of all Strads. In 1775, the maker's son Paolo sold it to Count Salabue, who kept it in its case until 1827, when he exchanged it with Tarisio for a Strad that had been made under the tutelage of Amati. The Messiah is thought to be completely untouched, except for an unfortunate change in the angle of the neck and replacement of the fingerboard and bass bar made by Vuillaume. Today it is part of the collection bequeathed to the Ashmolean Museum at Oxford by Hill, the famous London maker.

Although each of the great luthiers customarily made all the stringed instruments, certain makers had particular success with cellos; and to them we will give special attention.

To the best of our knowledge, the first luthier known to make cellos was Andrea Amati, (c. 1505–c. 1580), founder both of an important dynasty of luthiers and of the Cremonese School. Of beautiful workmanship, his instruments were similar in design to the ones we have today. His cellos in particular are richly sonorous; and their

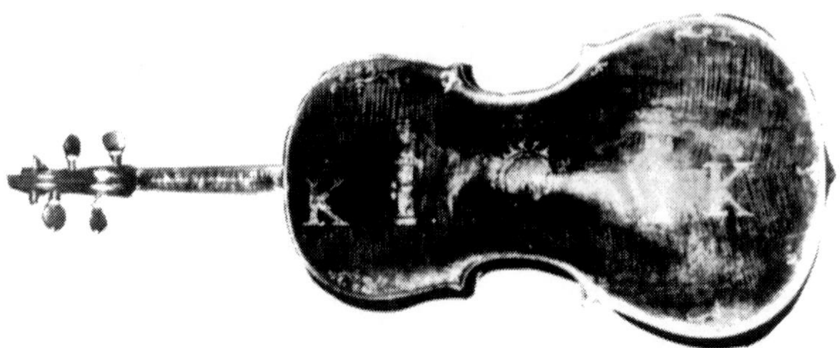

Figure 22. One of the earliest cellos in existence, made about 1570. This example of the Charles IX Andrea Amati set belongs to the Belgian baroque virtuoso Wieland Kuijken.

sound can fill even our modern concert halls, large as they are. Amati's immense reputation spread far beyond Italy. During the reign of Charles IX—very likely through the influence of Catherine de Medici—the French Court commissioned him to make a special group of instruments to form a royal orchestra: twenty-four violins (twelve large and twelve small), six violas, and eight cellos. Superb examples of the craftsmanship of the age, their backs and sides were richly decorated with the French coat of arms and the motto *PIETATE ET IVSTITIA*. These instruments were housed in the royal chapel at Versailles until 1790. During the French Revolution, they disappeared from the chateau; but since then, eight of them have been found—three violins, one viola, and four cellos. One of the cellos, known as the "King," is definitely dated 1572 and may be the oldest surviving cello, although another is possibly from 1569 (*Figure 22*). On the peg box of the "King" is the outline of a fifth hole, which suggests that it originally was a five-stringed cello.[5]

Gasparo di Bertolotti or Gasparo de Salo (1540–1609) is generally considered the founder of the Brescia School, which never became as prestigious as that of Cremona but nevertheless produced some excellent luthiers. At the present time, there are no authenticated cellos of

5. Laurence C. Witten II, "The Surviving Instruments of Andrea Amati," *Early Music* (October 1982).

this maker—examples carrying his signature being violas da gamba and transformed double basses. His handiwork is a little coarse, but it demonstrates a certain vigor that is not without beauty. The woods are well chosen, the varnish is rich, and the tone is powerful.

In the making of cellos, de Salo's pupil Giovanni-Paolo Maggini (1580–1632) was probably his superior. His design was better proportioned and very original. He made innovations in wood cutting and construction and notably in the way he treated the corners of his instruments. As a rule, he inlaid two parallel purflings as well as some ornaments in the middle of the back. His *f*-holes, which he designed with rare beauty, were placed rather low on his violins and high on his few cellos. These last were of both the small and the large models, but all were of excellent workmanship and beautiful proportion.

With Nicolo Amati (1596–1684), grandson of Andrea and the most eminent representative of this famous family, we arrive at a level of quality that only Amati's disciple Stradivari would surpass. His instruments show proof of very careful research; and in following the evolution of his art, one perceives in his diverse changes a constant search for improvement and perfection. He worked with special care on the thickness of the wood. Like all instruments of the Amati dynasty, Nicolo's were made on the da chiesa scale, but most of them have subsequently been cut down. Amati cellos are highly valued by performers—Alfredo Piatti played one, and some of our best cellists use them today.

For a long period, the instruments of the Amati family were the most popular of all, and some noted soloists preferred them to those of Guarneri and even of Stradivari. Because all were modified—more or less—and none has come to us in its original state, a comparison is impossible. This does not change the fact that Antonio Stradivari (1644–1737)—also known as Antonius Stradivarius from the Latin signature on the labels he placed in all his instruments—was indisputably the greatest luthier of all.

To what can one attribute Stradivari's incredible reputation? Although certain masters—Guadagnini or Vuillaume—reached a high level in craftsmanship, choice of woods, and beauty of varnish and others—Guarneri del Gesu or Montagnana—produced instruments of a sonorous tone quality that could be preferred to that of a Stradivarius, no one constructed so many marvelous instruments successful both for their acoustical properties and for their beauty. It is the consistent and exceptional union of these two components that has made the name of Stradivari synonymous with perfection in string instrument making. His enormous production, estimated at about fifteen hundred instruments—violins, altos, tenors, cellos, guitars, harps, and others—displays a consistently high level of craftsmanship. The elegant quality of tone is recognizable by its range and warmth and the workmanship by its meticulous and aristocratic execution. In addition, although Stradivari never duplicated the same model and strove constantly to improve his work, all his instruments—from those of his apprenticeship to those he made at the age of ninety-three—show a remarkable consistency and the omnipresent stamp of a master.

Stradivari's genius was recognized immediately, and there was great demand for his instruments. One Flemish musician, Jean-Baptiste Volumier (1677–1728), who was attached to the court of King August II of Poland, waited in Cremona for three months in 1715 to take delivery of twelve violins the king had ordered. Contemporary documents give some idea of the esteem in which Stradivari's work was held. In his memoirs, Don Desiderio Arisi, a monk and a close friend of the luthier, tells this story:

> On May 12, 1701, Don Antonio Cavezudo, director of the private orchestra of Charles II of Spain, wrote a very flattering letter to Stradivari saying that, although he had accepted some bowed instruments from fine makers for different courts, he had never encountered any which possessed a tone quality so pure and beautiful as his.

A letter written to Stradivari in 1716 by Lorenzo Giustiniani, member of an illustrious Venetian family, makes this request:

> I hear from all sides that nowhere in the world today is there a maker of musical instruments who is as expert as you. Wishing to own, personally, a souvenir of so illustrious a man and so famous an artist, I write to ask if you could make a violin for me, in the fabrication of which you will employ all your talents, to the end that it is the best and most beautiful instrument possible.

On September 19, 1690, Stradivari received this testimonial from Marquess Bartolomeo Ariberti:

> The other day, I made a gift to His Highness Como III, Duke of Tuscany, of two violins and one cello which I had ordered from you, and I can assure you—to my great satisfaction—that he accepted them with more pleasure than I can say. The musicians of his orchestra, and they are excellent, have been unanimous in their high estimation of your instruments; they declare them perfect and say particularly that they have never heard a cello with so agreeable a tone. It is to the extreme care which you exercised in making these instruments that I am indebted for the flattering reception with which His Highness accepted my gift. At the same time, I hope the gift I have made will prove to you my high, personal esteem, and will have succeeded in making so eminent a person as His Highness cognizant of your great skill. I have no doubt he will procure numerous commissions for you from this big family. To prove what I have just said, I entreat you to begin immediately on two altos, one for the tenor part and the other for the contralto, which we need to complete our quintet.

The three instruments surviving from this quintet, including the cello, can be found today in Florence at the museum of the Conservatorio Cherubini.

Although Stradivari's reputation is great, little is known about his life. The date of his birth is contested by authorities although he himself gave his age on a few of his labels. Nevertheless, we know that he was a pupil of Nicolo Amati and that fourteen years after going into business for himself, he was able to pay the considerable sum of 7000 imperial lire for a small, three-story house in the center of Cremona. Orders flowed into his shop from everywhere—from the courts of Spain and England, from the Medicis, from wealthy prelates—all his customers paying high prices for his instruments, to the point where the expression "rich as Stradivari" became common. The master turned out successful work consistently throughout his career, but his most productive period occurred between 1700 and 1720. It was his "golden age."

Contrary to what certain authors have written, Stradivari did not "invent" the standard dimensions of the cello (G. P. Maggini had already built models of this size), but he did determine and establish faultless proportions. All the cellos he constructed before 1700 were of the large dimension; but from 1707 on, he settled on a model from which he rarely departed, except in the last years of his life. The proportions of that model were universally accepted by his contemporaries, and they have been the ideal and perfect standard to this day.

His first known cello was made in 1667, but it has been considerably altered. Originally it was probably an instrument of six strings, like the Amati instruments discussed later. His last, the "Mendelssohn" (also known as the "Paganini"), was made in 1736. In the seventy intervening years, he probably produced about 150 cellos, of which only 63 survive.[6] Of these, some are more remarkable than others, and most of them are in a beautiful state of conservation. Each of these marvels constructed when his art had already reached its zenith has usually been named either for the personage who owned it at one time or for the celebrated virtuoso who played it. For example, there are the "Duport," the "General Kyd," the "Romberg," and others. I have had the good fortune to play a large number of these instruments, and I found it a joy to put a bow to their strings and draw from them tones whose unique quality is always recognizable, while at the same time each instrument retains its individual characteristics. I will not try to classify them for quality, as my judgment would be subjective in all cases; but my personal preference tends toward the following: the "Batta," the "Duport," the "Piatti," the "Suggia," the "de Munck," the "Davidov," the "Romberg," and the "Markevitch."

Alexander Batta (1816–1902), a French cellist of Belgian origin, owned a beautiful Amati cello of which he was very proud. It is said that one day in Paris he met Servais, who insisted that Batta accompany him to a violin shop where he had found a Strad cello dated 1714, which had, according to him, the most beautiful tone in the world. Batta reluctantly allowed himself to be persuaded; but after

6. Herbert K. Goodkind, *Violin Iconography of Antonio Stradivari* (Larchmont, N.Y., 1972).

seeing the instrument and playing a few notes, he literally fell in love with it. With the aid of a friend, he acquired it immediately and kept it, in spite of many opportunities to sell, until his seventy-eighth year, when it was taken over by the Hill family of London. Little is known about the instrument's history before 1836, except that it was in Madrid. Over the years, it has been in the collection of Baron Knoop of London and in that of Horace Havemeyer of New York. It was finally bought by Gregor Piatigorsky, who already owned another superb Strad—the "Baudiot" of 1725—which he used the most frequently. Previous to that, he had owned the "Lord Aylesford," dated 1696, which was a large model—intact until 1968 when its size was thoughtlessly cut down.

Piatigorsky had great respect for the "Batta." He considered its resources limitless; and while using it, he always tried for the perfection it deserved. On one of my last visits with him, he asked:

"Mitia, have you ever tried the Batta?"

"No."

"Then go take it out of its case."

I then had the immense honor of playing this cello, whose tone is pure musical honey. These few cherished moments will always remain with me.

Another Stradivarius cello, also of beautiful quality, is the "Duport," made in 1711. Vuillaume, the great French luthier of the last century, considered it a perfect example and made many copies of it. Stradivari made it for a doctor from Lyon, who paid double the usual price in order to be sure of getting an exceptional instrument. When the doctor died, it was put up for sale in Paris, but no buyer was found. The cellist Jean-Louis Duport was the only one to appreciate its quality; and some time later, he became its happy owner. When he died, his son, also a cellist, inherited it; but being a poor businessman, he was obliged to sell it in 1842. August Franchomme bought it for 22,000 francs—ten times the price Duport had paid—and he, too, cherished it all his life. Like the "Batta," the "Duport" eventually became part of Baron Knoop's collection in London and eventually passed into the hands of Horace Havemeyer. In 1969, it became the property of Gerald Warburg, an American amateur cellist

Figure 23. Mstislav Rostropovitch. *Photograph by Bob Martin.*

at whose house I had the opportunity to try it. I later played it at the home of Mstislav Rostropovitch, who has owned it since 1974 (*Figure 23*).

The great Italian cellist Alfredo Piatti found the cello that bears his name in Ireland. A magnificent instrument dated 1720, it was taken to Dublin in 1818 by a dealer returning from the war in Spain. In 1867, a wealthy Irish amateur gave it to Piatti. When he died, it went to the Mendelssohn family of bankers. Made by Stradivari when he was seventy-eight, it is a lovely specimen of his work in a perfect state of conservation.

While in Portugal on one of my earliest tours, I met Madame Suggia, who invited me to play (and to take tea) at her home. During my visit, she let me first try a magnificent Montagnana and then play her beautiful Stradivarius of 1717, which is depicted in the famous portrait of Suggia by Augustus John (*see Figure 48*). She used it on all her tours, for she highly valued its large, sonorous quality. I, too, admired it and was pleased to see it again, much later, in a large Swiss collection.

Emanuel Feuermann's instrument was constructed by Stradivari after 1730, near the end of his life. It is unique: it is the smallest he ever made, and its dimensions are untouched. It carries the name of Ernest de Munck (1840–1915), a renowned Belgian artist, who acquired it in 1869. Shortly thereafter, it passed into the hands of Franchomme, who kept it until his death in 1884. The tone of this cello is wonderfully free; it speaks easily and has good carrying power. One can still admire its sound on the recordings Feuermann left us. It was later bought by the Brazilian cellist Aldo Parisot, who let me play it several times.

In the section devoted to Karl Davidov, I tell how he received a superb Stradivarius of 1712 from Count Vielgorsky in 1870. The count had obtained this instrument from his friend Count Apraxine—another excellent cellist—in exchange for a Guarneri, 40,000 francs, and the best horse in his stable. Unfortunately, it fared badly in Davidov's possession. He played it a great deal, but apparently without discretion. Of the same model as the "Duport," it has a beautiful reddish-orange varnish. It was one of the instruments commissioned by the Duke of Tuscany.

Another beautiful Stradivarius—made in 1711—was owned by the excellent cellist Bernhard Romberg. It is unique, having only one black strip in the purfling instead of the usual two black and one white. In addition, its back and sides are made of poplar, a relatively ordinary wood compared to the maple normally used. Romberg adored this cello and felt that nothing could ever take the place of a Strad.

Still another lovely specimen, this one from 1709, is the "Markevitch" (*Figure 24*). In 1822, Andrei Gudovitch acquired it in exchange for a superb open carriage with four jet-black horses, as well as two bondsmen, a coachman, a footman, and all their families. Two years earlier, Alessandro Delfini of Brescia, solo cellist at La Scala in Milan, had brought it to Russia to sell. Gudovitch kept it until 1863, when he gave it to his grandnephew and godson, Senator Andrei Nicolaievitch Markevitch, an amateur cellist, an enthusiast, and director of the Russian Musical Society (*Figure 25*). Markevitch, my great uncle, was an active chamber musician to whom several com-

Figure 24. The "Markevitch" cello. This Stradivarius was made in 1709 during the great maker's golden period and is listed by Hill among the master's notable instruments. Of interest is the mark in the middle of the back left by a button used to carry it in processions.

posers, among them Popper, Tanieiev, and Napravnik, dedicated their works (*Figure 26*). His cello is apparently a church instrument: a sign of the button from which it was suspended for use in processions is still visible in the middle of the back. For many years, I have played it in my concerts.

Considering the prices reached at recent auctions for these instruments, one has trouble imagining that Cervetto, who brought some Stradivarius cellos to London in 1728, was unable to obtain a mere five pounds for them, and had to return them unsold to Italy. Pushed by inflation, a speculative fever has significantly affected the market for these violins and cellos, raising prices in a breathtaking manner and often putting them out of the reach of musicians. Many instruments finally fall into the hands of people who buy them as investments, rather than as works of art whose prime need and function are to be used to produce music.

Figure 25. Senator Andrei Nicolaievitch Markevitch (1830–1907) in full regalia. Jurist, amateur cellist, and patron of the arts, he was a prominent member of the Russian Senate.

Figure 26. Senator A. N. Markevitch in Moscow at the turn of the century, playing chamber music on his Stradivarius in the company of his friends. Seated in the background (second from the left)—the man with the pointed beard and mustache—is the author's father.

Without question, the cellos of Stradivari are of exceptional quality; but because of their strong personalities, they are instruments that can lead their players and become difficult to control. For this reason, certain artists—including Casals—have preferred instruments made by less famous luthiers but easier to control. Many of these cellos are beautiful; and although their makers are not so universally renowned as Stradivari, they deserve to be mentioned. The following list names some of the great Italian luthiers in chronological order by year of birth. Heading the list are members of the Ruggieri and Rogeri families, whose names are frequently confused.

Francesco Ruggieri, il per, (1645–1700).

Vincenzo Ruggieri (1690–1735).

Giovanni Battista Rogeri (c. 1650–c. 1730).

Pietro Giacomo Rogeri (c. 1680–1730), one of whose instruments belonged to Paganini.

David Tecchler (1666–1743), a distinguished luthier originally from the Tyrol, who settled in Rome. He fashioned his models after the styles of Amati and Stainer. Certain artists have liked his cellos very much. My first teacher, Maurice Eisenberg, owned a superb one from 1712, and for a long time I have played a beautiful example, dated 1713, on my tours.

Giovanni Grancino (1675–1737), a Milanese maker whose instruments have a penetrating tone, well suited to the concert halls of today.

Matteo Goffriler (1690–1742), who worked in Venice. He is known particularly for his cellos, which usually have a beautiful, strong, and resonant tone. Casals had one that he particularly liked.

Domenicò Montagnana (1690–1750), who was especially successful. A disciple of Stradivari, he followed his master in modeling his instruments but made them more massive. Their woods are well chosen, the scrolls and *f*-holes are admirably cut, and the varnish is of a beautiful, rich quality. Their tone is round, warm, and strong. During a great part of his career, Gregor Piatigorsky used a magnificent specimen made by this Venetian master in 1739.

Giuseppe Guarneri, del Gesu (1698–1744), one of a large family of makers in Cremona. He is known as *del Gesu* because he added the eucharistic sign IHS to his signature. His superb instruments are less refined in workmanship than those of Stradivari; but they are nevertheless preferred by many eminent violinists, who especially like the power and richness of their exceptional tone. Unlike Stradivari, Guarneri did not work for the nobility and aristocracy; and his production was relatively small. About fifty violins and only one cello, dated 1739, have come down to us. The origin of the cello is contested by some authorities, but it is probably authentic. Consequently, cellists can only lament that this genius did not create more for us.

Giovanni Battista Guadagnini (1711–1786), who worked in Cremona, Parma, and Turin. He turned out instruments noted for their fine craftsmanship. His cellos are frequently small, but they always carry the stamp of a true master, and their sonority is full and warm.

Francesco Pressenda (1777–1854), a disciple of Guadagnini, known especially for his cellos.

Giuseppi Antonio Rocca (1807–1865), apprenticed to Pressenda, whose cellos are likewise admired.

Giuseppi Scarampella (1838–1885), a producer of lovely and original instruments. In 1877, however, he was inspired for no good reason to reduce the proportions of a beautiful Stradivarius of 1690, still in its original state and formerly part of a quintet belonging to Ferdinand de Medici, duke of Tuscany.

In Germany, *Jacob Stainer* (c. 1617–1683) was the best representative of the indigenous school. Of him John Hawkins wrote in his *General History of the Science and Practice of Music* (London, 1776), "The instruments from Cremona are surpassed only by those of Stainer." His art is characterized mainly by the high body-arching of his instruments and by scrolls carved in the shape of animal heads. In Mittenwald, Germany's center of instrument making, we find the important *Klotz* family, whose members have been producing from the end of the seventeenth century to the present time.

William Forster (1739–1806), *Thomas Dodd* (1760–c. 1820), and *John F. Lott* (1775–1853), were all English luthiers who made some interesting cellos.

In France, the nineteenth century school of violin making was regarded highly, in particular for its fine cellos, which possess a remarkable resonance. The first noted French maker was *Nicolas Lupot* (1758–1824). He was followed by *Jean-Baptiste Vuillaume* (1798–1875), whose production was enormous (about 3000 instruments, most of which are numbered), but he made only about thirty cellos. Vuillaume made many copies of the models of other makers, some so perfect they were mistaken for the originals. For these, the "Duport" Stradivarius was his favorite model. From the French school, one can also cite *Gand*, *Bernadel*, *Lété*, and *Miremont*.

In the unanimous opinion of his colleagues, the best luthier of our century was *Simone Fernando Sacconi* (1890–1973). He began his apprenticeship in Italy at the age of eight and quickly became famous. He soon moved to New York, where he spent the largest part of his life. One of his cellos, a copy of a Stradivarius, which I have tried sounded remarkably well. He is the author of *I Segreti di Stradivari*, published in Cremona in 1972.

Figure 27. Makoto Toba, a young Suzuki student from Matsumoto, Japan, is learning to play cello at the Talent Education School. *Photograph by Hubert Le Campion.*

The Performers

PRODIGIES YOUNG AND OLD

A CELLO CAN BE PLAYED by a young child, providing the size of the instrument is adapted to the size of the child, and by a very old person as well, since its player is sitting down.

At present, particularly in Japan, the cello is taught to children as young as four years old using the precepts of Shinichi Suzuki. This remarkable method of training, which has been producing good results for many years, was originally conceived for the violin; but it has been adapted to the cello, the viola, and even to the piano and flute (*Figure* 27.)

Child prodigies have always attracted the attention of the public. One of the first of these, Benjamin Hallet appeared at London's new Haymarket Theatre in 1749. He was only six years old and he was either dressed as a little girl in a gown with petticoats or made up to represent Cupid; but when he played his cello solos, he drew much applause (*Figure* 28). In the 1770s, a Polish prodigy named Nicholas Zygmuntowski made a grand tour of Europe at the age of seven. He performed successfully in Paris, and the *Journal de Paris* said of him, "He plays with the utmost accuracy, observes precisely the pianos and fortes, and generally everything is done with taste and given musical expression."

Figure 28. Portrait of Benjamin Hallet by Thomas Jenkins showing the young prodigy dressed as a girl for his concerts. Engraving (c. 1750) by James McArdell.

The world of the cello embraces not only the prodigy but the long-lived as well. One of the earliest English cellists we know of, Bartholomew Johnson, was born in 1710. In 1810, he gracefully played a minuet he had composed sixty years earlier at a banquet in honor of his one-hundredth birthday (*Figure 29*). Johnson lived to be 104, a record among cellists, although there are documents showing that the Italian cellist Giacomo Basevi (known as Cervetto) lived from 1682 to 1783. In our own day, Pablo Casals played the cello until the year of his death at the age of 97, working at it regularly every day (*Figure 30*).

THE NATIONAL SCHOOLS AND THE GREAT PERFORMERS

PABLO CASALS

Throughout most of his long life Pablo Casals (1876–1973) was a world renowned performer, whose pioneering musical style and unusual life never ceased to amaze. In 1913, his exploits as a tennis

Figure 29 (left). Bartholomew Johnson (1710–1814). A contemporary engraving of the portrait painted to celebrate his one-hundredth birthday.
Figure 30 (right). Casals at ninety in 1966—still strong and happy, and still playing the cello.

player in the Musicians' Tournament were watched with great excitement (*Figure 31*). During the Spanish Civil War of the 1930s, he called the world's attention to the problems of Spain by leaving his native country and going into voluntary exile at Prades in the Pyrenees. From that base, he organized and dispensed help for Spanish refugees. In 1945, he announced his decision to protest against world tyranny by withdrawing from all public appearances as an artist. Eventually, he agreed to play at the Festival of Prades, which was founded in his honor in 1950. Beginning in 1957, he played annually at the Casals Festival in Puerto Rico, where he spent the rest of his life. It was also in 1957 that he surprised the world by announcing his third formal marriage. His new bride was Martita Montanez, one of his pupils, who was exactly sixty years his junior.

This man—short, bald, timid of appearance, even clumsy, the opposite of a Spanish musical-comedy type—was nonetheless the center of many colorful episodes. In 1913, at the Colonne Concerts in

Figure 31. On 22 June 1913, Casals competed in the Musicians' Tennis Championship in Paris. He is on the right in the white hat. With him, from left to right, are composer W. Bastard, pianist Maurice Dumesnil, and composer E. Chelli.

Paris, he created a scandal by refusing to play the Dvořák Cello Concerto under the direction of Gabriel Pierné. At the rehearsal, Pierné, a composer as well as a conductor, offended Casals deeply by asserting that Dvořák's music was so wretched it was not worth the trouble of a rehearsal. A bailiff was called to the premises, who later confirmed the definite refusal of the artist to participate in the concert. Casals lost the ensuing lawsuit and was fined 3000 francs, a formidable amount for those days. So it is, good taste is not always predominant in the eyes of the law.

At the beginning of the century during one of his first American tours, an impresario tried to prevail on Casals to conceal his baldness with a toupée, hoping thus to increase the price of the tickets. Casals vehemently refused. Meanwhile, he was stupefied to read in a newspaper that his baldness was the result of having given a lock of his hair to each of his paramours.

Born at Vendrell in Catalonia, Pablo Casals played the flute, the violin, and various other instruments before devoting himself solely to the cello. Although for the most part he was self-taught, he did attend some classes at the Barcelona Conservatory, chiefly in counterpoint and chamber music. At about the same time, he studied violoncello for a few months with Josep Garcia, nephew of Manuel Garcia, the famous singer of the last century.

At the age of thirteen he found a copy of the Suites for unaccompanied cello by Johann Sebastian Bach while browsing in a music shop. This discovery was a great revelation to him. The suites were almost unknown at that time, and they were rarely played in their entirety (although isolated sections were sometimes used as solo pieces). Almost twenty years later, Casals established the custom of presenting them as complete units. In 1909, a critic from Hamburg penned a review typical of the reaction in musical circles of that time:

> After having performed the Schumann Concerto, Pablo Casals played something very surprising. Imagine a cello being played alone, without accompaniment, in the huge Laishalle! That seemed curious at first, but while listening to him play the Suite in C major of J. S. Bach, one was very quickly captivated.

Meanwhile, violinists like Eugene Ysaye had been influenced by this mode of presentation and began to perform Bach's sonatas and partitas for solo violin in their entirety.

In his search for an eloquent interpretation of these suites, Casals considerably modified the cello's technique, a skill that had become rigid and unchanging in the previous century. He sought to liberate the interpreter from the mechanical aspects of playing and thus allow him to concentrate solely on the exposition of musical ideas; and his instincts frequently led him to discover new methods of execution. One of his favorite principles was what he called "expressive intonation," a principle more supple and more natural, and more responsive and sensitive to harmonic progressions and melodic lines. His interpretations, however, were not always universally appreciated. One English critic said of him, "Casals has a spirit so scholastic he can play only in a scholastic manner."

In 1898, his debut in Paris at the Concerts Lamoureux was a great success. His interpretation of the Lalo Concerto impressed the audience with its simplicity of style, which stood in marked contrast to the manner of his contemporaries, whose taste was often questionable. The occasion began a great international career, which Casals pursued for seventy-four years, sometimes playing as many as 250 concerts in one year.

Casals also participated in numerous trio recitals with Alfred Cortot and Jacques Thibaud, a combination that became one of the most celebrated in musical history. In 1919, Casals took part in founding the École Normale de Musique in Paris, where he continued as a director and teacher. The following year, he founded the Orquesta Pau Casals in Barcelona, a group that became so well trained and well respected that well-known soloists were proud to appear with it. Sources of particular pride to Casals were the series of concerts he organized for the workers and the performance of Beethoven's Ninth Symphony he gave on the occasion of the birth of the Spanish Republic. He wrote music steadily during his life, but most of his works are unpublished, except for his oratorio *El Pessebre*, which was given worldwide performances in 1962.

THE STUDENTS OF CASALS

Although he had a number of important students, few ever attained international recognition. One exception was his first wife, the talented Portuguese cellist Guilhermina Suggia (*See Figure* 48). During the few years of their tumultuous marriage, Casals and Suggia gave many joint concerts, playing works for two cellos composed especially for them. Another student was Gaspar Cassadó (1897–1966) who had the biggest career of all the disciples of Casals. Unfortunately, political beliefs and emotions inflamed by the Spanish Civil War alienated him from Casals, and the latter disavowed him. He is remembered for many brilliant compositions still in the cello repertoire and memorialized by the Prix Cassadó, an award recognizing talented young cellists which was established in his memory in Florence, the city where he lived for many years.

Figure 32. Maurice Eisenberg taught cello from 1930 to 1939 at the Paris École Normale de Musique. He was an excellent and enthusiastic teacher, whose classes were always exciting.

But the pupil Casals regarded almost as an adopted son was Maurice Eisenberg (1900–1972), an American who had a brilliant career as both a soloist and a teacher (*Figure 32*). Eisenberg profited greatly from the tutelage of eminent professors such as Julius Klengel, Hugo Becker, and Diran Alexanian. Following his first concert in Paris in 1926, he met Casals, and becoming one of his most fervent disciples, eventually succeeded him as professor at l'École Normale de Musique in Paris. After 1939, he remained in the United States, where he taught at the Longy School of Music in Cambridge, Massachusetts, and then at the Juilliard School in New York. He was frequently invited to give courses at the major American universities and conservatories. His book *Cello Playing of Today*, published in 1957, is a resumé of his pedagogical precepts, which are based on the interpretations of Casals and on his own experiences. Eisenberg was my first instructor, and I still remember the day he introduced me to Casals (I must have been about eight) saying, "Maestro, here is a young cellist who would like to play like you someday." To which Casals responded, "I would hope, rather, that he will play like himself." I have never forgotten this wish.

FRANCESCO ALBOREA (FRANCISCELLO)

Actually, Casals was a spontaneous phenomenon who belonged to no scholastic tradition. In this he was unlike other great artists of the twentieth century such as Gregor Piatigorsky and Emanuel Feuermann, whose musical heritage can be traced back to Francesco Alborea (1691–1739), more commonly known as Franciscello. *Figure 33* traces his pervasive influence. The impact of Alborea on his epoch was remarkable. People traveled from Rome—even from as far away as Vienna—just to hear him play. The great Neapolitan composer Alessandro Scarlatti (1660–1725), who played with him frequently, thought that "only an angel can play in this way" and wrote three sonatas in his honor. Perhaps Scarlatti also had him in mind when he wrote difficult technical passages for the cello in some of his cantatas, which, according to his contemporaries, Franciscello surmounted with the utmost ease. On a visit to Naples, from Prussia, J. J. Quantz, Frederick II's court musician and flute teacher, deemed him "incomparable."

Under the patronage of the amateur cellist Count von Uhlenfeld, Franciscello went to Vienna, where he met many celebrities (*Figure 34*). Among these was the violinist Franz Benda (1709–1786), the first of a dynasty of famous musicians, who said he was so affected by Franciscello's playing that he completely revised his own technique and adopted the other's style.

MARTIN BERTEAU

Because of his wonderful reputation, Franciscello was credited with a huge number of students—so many, in fact, that some are obviously apocryphal (*See Figure 33*). It is thought that Martin Berteau (1709–1771), who became one of the founders of the French school of cello, must have studied with him. In any case, Berteau was so greatly influenced by Franciscello's skill that he decided to abandon his chosen instrument—the viola da gamba—and take up the cello. His progress seems to have been rapid because as early as 1739 he appeared at the Concert Spirituel. This was a musical organization that

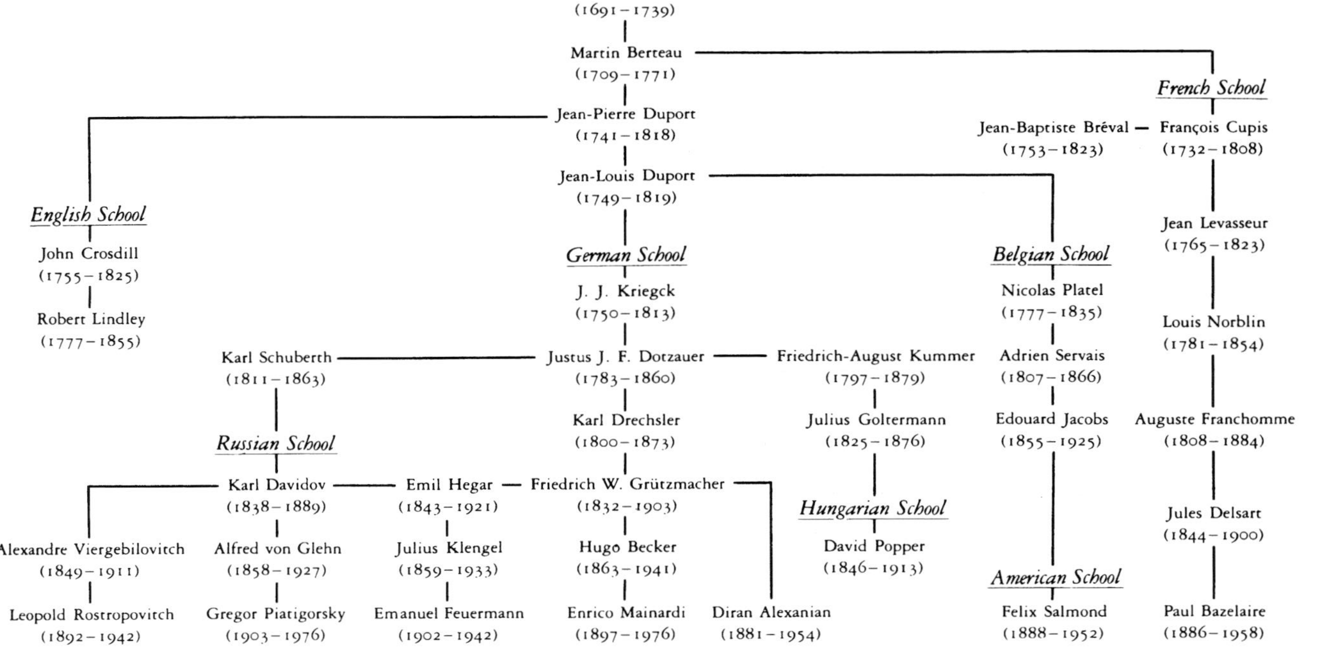

Figure 33. The long bow of Franciscello.

Figure 34. Franciscello (1691–1739), whose real name was Francesco Alborea. During his engagement at the Austrian Imperial Chapel, he commanded the highest salary ever paid to a cellist. The contemporary portrait by Martin Meiten of Vienna in an engraving by Jacob Haid.

flourished from 1725 to 1789, which was instrumental in the formation of the prevailing musical taste. It was devoted to furthering the recognition of composers of instrumental music and to publicizing the best performers as well: "The most renowned virtuosi of Europe take turns coming there to shine." To achieve success before this august body was the supreme ambition of any artist. When Berteau played some of his own works there, he was received enthusiastically, his beautiful tone and deep expressiveness winning considerable praise. In *The Age of Louis XV* (Paris, 1753), the following tribute can be found: "No person could ever hope to have more fire than Berteau." It is possible that his immoderate taste for good wine, which he called his "rosin," added to this artistic warmth.

JEAN-PIERRE DUPORT

Berteau was a well known teacher. Among his many students were François Cupis (1732–1808) and Jean-Pierre Duport (1741–1818), called Duport the Elder to distinguish him from his younger brother Jean-Louis, who would eventually become the more celebrated of the two. On the occasion of a triumphal appearance at the Concert Spirituel, Jean-Pierre's talent was praised in this glowing review from *Mercure de France* (April 1762):

> M. Duport repeatedly exhibits new marvels on the cello and earns renewed admiration. In his hands the instrument is unrecognizable: it speaks, it expresses, it conveys everything—with an enchantment greater than that which was always thought to be the exclusive property of the violin.
>
> The agility of his execution is always accompanied by the most exact accuracy in passages of technical difficulty—difficulty which no one can imagine without a thorough knowledge of the instrument. It is unanimously agreed today that this young man is the most singular phenomenon to have appeared among the most talented. One cannot foresee anything he could add to the degree of perfection he has attained.

In 1769, Duport gave up his position in the orchestra of the Prince de Conti and toured France, England, and Spain. It is said that one day, while passing through a small town on his way to a city where he was to perform, he noticed a great many posters announcing a concert for that very evening with him as the featured player. Impelled by curiosity and determined to get to the bottom of the matter, he went to the theatre at the stated hour. There he found a large audience, undoubtedly attracted by his name, which was already widely known. As the concert began, Duport watched stupefied as an unknown cellist came on stage and confidently began the first number. But it was soon evident that his playing was far below the standard of perfection of a big artist, and the audience rapidly showed its dissatisfaction. When the situation began to grow menacing, Duport could restrain himself no longer. He approached the stage, introduced himself, and seizing the instrument from the poor impostor, finished the concert to the applause and bravos of an ecstatic audience. At the end of the evening, the impostor offered Duport the sizable receipts from the ticket sales, which had been swelled by the use of his famous name. But the celebrated musician refused to take it. He felt that the disgrace the unfortunate cheat had suffered was punishment enough.

In 1773, he arrived in Berlin, where he was to live until his death in 1818. There, Frederick II engaged him as solo cellist for the Royal Chapel and for the Opera. He also taught the Crown Prince, the future Frederick-William II. When the prince became king in 1786, he appointed Duport to the post of Music Superintendent to the Royal Chamber, which he filled until 1806. At a concert in this court in 1796 Duport took part in the première of Beethoven's first two Sonatas for cello and piano, opus 5, with the composer himself at the piano. Duport's own compositions, which were mostly for the cello, were so popular that Mozart used a theme from one of the minuets in his Variations for piano, K. 575.

JEAN-LOUIS DUPORT

Of all Duport's great qualities, the beauty and fullness of his tone were those he most successfully transmitted to his pupils. Among these were the Englishman John Crosdill and his own brother Jean-Louis Duport (1749–1819), who would someday eclipse his older brother, great as his reputation was (*Figure* 35). Duport the younger began as a violinist, but he quickly devoted himself solely to the cello. At the age of nineteen, with his brother providing the accompaniment, Jean-Louis made his debut at the Concert Spirituel, where he enjoyed an immediate and brilliant success. The Prince of Guémènée, an amateur cellist, engaged him at once to play in his orchestra and to give him lessons. He was all the rage with the important musical societies of the day and was offered more engagements than he could accept. In 1783, at the invitation of his friend and confrere, John Crosdill, he went to London, where he caused a sensation with his style and technique.

Sometime later, history places Jean-Louis Duport at the Court of Versailles on an occasion when Marie-Antoinette asked the famed Italian violinist Giovanni Battista Viotti to play one of his compositions. Viotti was late, and as the assemblage grew tired of waiting for him, Duport asked permission to look at the violin part. Taking his

Figure 35. Jean-Louis Duport playing in thumb position (probably on his Stradivarius) using a pre-Tourte type bow which he holds well beyond the frog. This lovely oil portrait (c. 1785) by the French court painter Madame Vigée-Lebrun is in the collection of the author.

cello, he read it perfectly—at sight—reaping the praise of the queen and others in the audience, all of whom were highly impressed.

In many aspects, Duport was greatly influenced by Viotti. Spurred on by his example, he searched for innovations in cello technique, and his discoveries eventually gave such an impetus to the artistic development of the instrument that critics dubbed him the "Viotti of the violoncello." It was inevitable that these two artists would play together frequently.

While in Geneva to give a concert, Duport called on Voltaire, who was living in retirement at Ferney, a short distance away. He played for the philosopher and won the following commentary (Voltaire actually knew very little about music): "Monsieur Duport, you make me believe in miracles, you know how to make a nightingale out of an ox."

Fleeing from the French Revolution in 1789, Jean-Louis joined his brother in Berlin. He was warmly welcomed and immediately given a position at the Prussian Royal Chapel, which he held until the invasion by the Napoleonic army in 1806. During the next few years, he stayed in Marseilles in the service of the Spanish King Charles IV, who was living there in exile. He then returned to Paris; and in 1813, he became professor at the Conservatory and solo cellist at the Imperial Chapel.

An apocryphal anecdote from this period tells of a meeting between Duport and Napoleon. During one of the "Concerts Intimes" at the Tuileries, in which Duport often participated, Napoleon entered, dressed in hunting clothes complete with spurs on his boots. After listening to the music for a bit and manifesting some satisfaction, the Emperor took the cello from Duport's hands, sat down, and demanded, "M. Duport, how do you hold this gadget?" He then clasped the magnificent Stradivarius between his knees; but in doing so, he carelessly inflicted a huge scratch on it with his spurs. Seeing his priceless instrument thus mistreated, poor Duport could not refrain crom crying out in a tortured voice, "Sire!" Rather than being offended, Napoleon was moved by this spontaneous reaction immediately to return the cello to its owner. (The history of this cello is related in the chapter on luthiers.)

Duport was a man of simplicity and generosity, traits his enormous talent and great success did not spoil. In the preface to his "Éssai sur le doigte du violoncelle et la conduite de l'archet (Essay on the Fingering of the Cello and the Conduct of the Bow"), he shows habitual modesty in his reference to his brother, Jean-Pierre: "to him who was, is, and always will be my master." His name will always be associated with this essay, which was published about 1805 and laid down the foundation of modern technique. For his epoch, this work presented an entirely new conception of the techniques for both hands. Many of its precepts are still considered valid and respected by modern cellists, while the twenty-one exercises that conclude this method are used regularly by students of today. Many of his pupils became the founders of different national schools of cello playing, and some of their descendents are among the fine cellists of our time (*See Figure 33*).

JUSTUS DOTZAUER

In Paris, Duport had a pupil named J. J. Kriegck (1750–1813), who eventually returned to his home town of Meiningen where he became Kapellmeister of the Court. His greatest achievement there was becoming the teacher of Justus Dotzauer (1783–1860), an important member of the German school and the founder of the school for cello in Dresden. To many young cellists, the name Dotzauer stands for the bogey-man who dreamed up those daily tortures—called Etudes—which are inflicted on them, often to an exaggerated degree. But among his contemporaries, musicians such as Ludwig Spohr, the celebrated violinist and composer, admired him greatly for his interpretive skill, the purity of his intonation, and the perfection of his technique.

Dotzauer made his debut at the age of 15 playing the Pleyel Variations and afterward studied with Romberg in Berlin. Primarily an orchestral musician, he played for several years in the Leipzig Orchestra and then occupied the solo cello position in the orchestra of the Dresden Court from 1821 to 1850. He was also an excellent chamber musician, often playing quartets with Spohr and other leading artists. In addition, he found time to give many concerts throughout Germany, Austria, and Holland and to compose many works for cello—as well as an opera, several symphonies, a mass, and some chamber music. His major contribution nevertheless was to pedagogy. He wrote several study methods and nearly two hundred etudes and exercises that are still valid. Some of his pupils became well known, the most famous being F. A. Kummer, Karl Schuberth, and Karl Drechsler.

FRIEDRICH GRÜTZMACHER

Along with Romberg, Dotzauer can be considered a patriarch of those German cellists who came to dominate the European musical scene in the nineteenth century. Their influence continued through the work of the cellists they taught, and it is still felt today. An important representative of this school was Friedrich Grützmacher (1832–1903), (whose name can be translated as *mushmaker*), a student of Karl Drechsler. Unfortunately, he is best remembered for the multitude of questionable transcriptions of masterworks for cello which he made—editions that are more like paraphrases but continue to defile our ears. In 1884 Peters, the big publishing house in Leipzig, rejected one of

Figure 36. Friedrich Wilhelm Grützmacher, the "Joan of Arc of the transcription," looked rather stern and humorless.

his arrangements because it was judged to be excessive. In reply, he wrote them an offended letter, which included these remarks:

> I could not have a more unhappy surprise than that contained in your letter. . . . A work which has been done on my part with the greatest care and love you regard as a failure? . . . Some great masters like Schumann and Mendelssohn have never taken the time to notate all the indications and nuances necessary, *down to the smallest detail*. . . . My main purpose has been to reflect and to determine what these masters might have been thinking, and to set down all that they, themselves, could have indicated. . . . Regarding this activity, and relying on my long musical experience, I feel *I have more right than all the others to do this work*. I have the approval of many renowned composers, but naturally, Schumann and Mendelssohn can no longer give theirs to me. . . . I do not fear the opinion they could have had because when one has had—as I—the opportunity to play all types of

> music often, there is not a doubt that he is capable of doing this kind of editing. . . . Schumann had no practical sense, so it is indispensible *not to correct* but to *complete* the nuances. . . . Who could possibly see anything in my work but a great deal of care and love, since it cannot be thought that it is done from a lack of knowledge. That would indeed be censurable. . . . PS My concert version of the Bach Suites, which you likewise mention, cannot also be a subject of reproach since, in editing them, I not only tried to follow the *same intentions* of which I have just spoken, but I succeeded at it. I have reaped much success in presenting this edition in concert, something that would have been impossible with the bare original in its primitive state.

One reads these lines with numb fascination. They prove that this "Joan of Arc of the transcription" believed he was destined to fulfill a great mission, with all the best intentions in the world. But the proverb "The road to hell is paved with good intentions" was never illustrated better.

Grützmacher—who, incidentally, looked rather like an English vicar, remains important because of the enormous number of cellists whom he trained in the Dotzauer school (*Figure* 36).

EMANUEL FEUERMANN

Jascha Heifetz is generally agreed to be the violinist who made the greatest mark on his time. His transcendental technique was without equal. Emanuel Feuermann (1902–1942), one year younger and—unfortunately for the musical world—dead before he reached forty, was his unchallenged counterpart as a cellist (*Figure* 37). In their lives as well as their playing, there are parallels between these two artists. Moreover, they often performed together, and some of their recordings, such as the Double Concerto of Brahms or the Mozart Divertimento in E$^{\flat}$ major K.563 with the fine violist William Primrose, remain with us as unequalled examples of their artistry.

Feuermann was born in Kolomiya, Galicia, near the Ukraine border. He was not yet six years old when his father gave him a cello and taught him the basic principles of playing it. Because his home town was so small, the family moved to Vienna to enable him to

Figure 37. The great cello virtuoso Emanuel Feuermann (1902–1942), despite his tragically brief life, has left us some splendid recordings.

continue his studies. His progress there was so rapid that he soon made his way to Leipzig, to study with the great teacher Julius Klengel.

Julius Klengel (1859–1933), who was born in Leipzig and lived there throughout his life, was a pupil of the Swiss cellist Emil Hegar, a disciple of Grützmacher. At the age of fifteen, he joined the Gewandhaus Orchestra and remained its principal cellist from 1881 to 1924. He taught at the Leipzig Conservatory, where he had the title of "Royal Professor." His numerous compositions included a Double Concerto for violin and cello, another for two cellos, and a remarkable Chaconne for unaccompanied cello. To his many pupils, all of whom adored him, he was warm and affectionate—treating them with a paternal kindness to which they responded fully. His most famous disciples besides Feuermann are Piatigorsky and Eisenberg.

One day, when Feuermann's parents asked Klengel to give an opinion of their son's playing, he responded, "I could still learn from him." This happened in the year Feuermann gave his first public concerts, when he was less than nine years old. After a recital in Vienna, one critic wrote, "This lad transfigures the music."

At the age of fourteen, Feuermann joined his brother, who was apparently a good violinist, in the Brahms Double Concerto, accompanied by the Berlin Philharmonic under the baton of Felix Weingartner. Two years later, he was named a professor of cello at the Cologne Conservatory; and in 1929, he was chosen to succeed Hugo Becker (1863–1941) as leading professor at the Hochschule für Musik in Berlin. Feuermann was the very opposite of his predecessor. Becker was cold and methodical, and his purely intellectual approach to music is evident from his work, *Mechanik und Asthetik aus Violoncellspiels* (1929). A student of Grützmacher and Piatti, Becker enjoyed a fairly successful career as a soloist. As a chamber musician, he formed a trio with Artur Schnabel and Karl Flesch; and he often played with Ysaye and Busoni.

The advent of Nazism forced Feuermann to leave Germany, and he emigrated to the United States, where his career took on new energy. He traveled in America and Europe, playing with the major orchestras under the most eminent conductors, and garnering enormous success everywhere.

As a child, I remember hearing Feuermann in recital at the Salle Gaveau in Paris. His facility, his freedom, and the natural way he expressed himself impressed me greatly. Although small in size, his 1730 Stradivarius, the "de Munck," vibrated under his fingers with a magnificent tone, and the purity and clarity of his execution was a true revelation.

His extensive repertoire covered all the cello literature available at that time, and he also pioneered new works. In 1936, he gave the initial performance of Arnold Schoenberg's Concerto. His deep admiration for Casals once led him to ask this artist what he did in a certain difficult passage of Haydn's D major Concerto. The great Spanish master replied, "I pray."

SOME ENGLISH CELLISTS

The cello emerged later in England than in other countries. Most of the first cellists there were foreigners, the majority being Italian: Cervetto père, Andrea Caporale, Pasqualini, and others, who arrived in London during the years following 1730. At this time, England was still the realm of the viola da gamba; and from 1760 until his death in 1787, Carl Friedrich Abel was its acknowledged king. Abel, who also played the cello, was a friend to Johann Christian Bach, son of Johann Sebastian Bach, and to the painter Gainsborough, whose sketches covered the walls of his apartment.

It was principally as an orchestral instrument that the cello was used in these days. Around 1603, the composer John Dowland designates it to "hold" the bass in his song "Lachrymae."

The first Englishman to make a reputation as a solo cellist was John Crosdill (1755–1825), who was already giving concerts at the age of nine. Crosdill nevertheless went to Paris to learn from Jean-Pierre Duport and other cellists from the flourishing French school. On his return to London, he was admitted to the best society and his brilliant career was launched. He became the leading cellist of the day and a reputable teacher. One of his pupils was the future King George IV. Another was Robert Lindley (1776–1855), who became the most important of the English cellists and the real founder of the English School. He too showed great aptitude for the instrument at an early age, and at nine he was a member of the orchestra of the Brighton Theatre. At twelve, he played for the prince of Wales, who was studying with Crosdill. The prince encouraged him to continue his lessons. He did, studying with Crosdill and Cervetto the younger. When he was eighteen, the latter obtained for him the position of first cellist in two orchestras, those of the King's Theatre and of the Italian Opera, posts he occupied for a record tenure of fifty-eight years. His schedule was overflowing: he participated regularly in Philharmonic Concerts, he played an incalculable number of chamber music concerts, and he became a professor at the Royal Academy in London from the time of its founding in 1822. His facility and his special talent for reading any kind of music at sight were legendary. Even Romberg, who was not often kind to his colleagues, said of Lindley after hearing him play one of Romberg's own concertos, "He is the devil!" Lindley had a longstanding friendship with the Italian double bass player, Domenico Dragonetti, a relationship that lasted almost fifty-two years. During this period, they gave many concerts together, playing duets in which their specialties were arrangements of Corelli violin sonatas. They also appeared very often before the Philharmonic Society of London, where they met with much success.

AUGUSTE FRANCHOMME

In the nineteenth century, the most attractive representative of the French school of cello was undoubtedly Chopin's close friend Auguste Franchomme (1808–1884) (*Figure 38*). This handsome, distinguished musician, with an elegance that is reflected in his compositions, collaborated with the illustrious Polish composer in several works. He took an active part in the musical life of Paris—occupying first chair in the orchestras of L'Opera and the Théatre des Italiens, and in 1846 becoming professor at the Conservatoire, where he had been a pupil of Jean Levasseur and Louis Norblin. These two masters had studied with Cupis, himself a student of the great Berteau, thus forming a lineal branch of the French School parallel to that of Duport. It is interesting to note that Franchomme bought Jean-Louis Duport's Stradivarius cello after the latter's death.

With the violinist Delphin Alard, a son-in-law of the luthier

Figure 38. The elegant French cellist Auguste Franchomme (1808–1884) wrote many interesting works for the cello, but most are still in manuscript.

Vuillaume, and the Anglo-German pianist Charles Halle, founder of the Manchester orchestra, Franchomme organized an important and popular series of chamber music concerts in Paris. In composing, he collaborated with George Osborne, Henri Bertini, and Chopin, with whom he was on friendly terms for many years. They worked together on a Grand Duo based on themes from Meyerbeer's *Robert le Diable*, Franchomme writing the cello part and Chopin the piano part. Although Chopin wrote an Introduction and Polonaise opus 3, which he dedicated to Joseph Merk during his visit to Vienna in 1830, there is another version of this work by Franchomme, which is more cellistic.

Franchomme's influence is also very apparent in Chopin's fine Sonata for cello and piano opus 65. It was his last composition, and he played it with Franchomme at his final concert, in the Salle Pleyel on February 16, 1848. On the manuscript, which is in the Bibliotheque Nationale in Paris, one can read the following inscription: "The cello part of the Sonata for cello and piano by Chopin was written out by me, at his dictation. Franchomme." Of the sonatas Chopin composed, this was the only one he himself ever performed in public. Conversely, one is aware that Franchomme tried to imitate the Chopin of the nocturnes, mazurkas, and etudes in his own compositions, especially in the Caprices opus 7, and the Etudes opus 34. In addition to these, his Concerto in C major opus 33, for cello and orchestra, is worthy of interest.

FRANÇOIS ADRIEN SERVAIS

Watching a cellist perform, one finds it entirely natural to see his instrument resting on the floor supported by the end-pin. This accessory has been in general use only since the closing years of the last century. To learn how players managed before that, let us look at cello methods of earlier times.

In his *Method* of 1741, Michel Corrette gives these precise details: "Observe that [the body of] the cello does not rest on the floor, with the result that it is muted; if the player has to stand up, one uses a peg to support the instrument; not only is this posture most unattractive but it is also most inhibiting in playing difficult passages."

In the *Method* of Raoul, published in 1797, the author says:

> It is necessary to sit forward on one's chair and to place the cello in such a way that the indented part on the left side of the back rests against the inside of the knee joint. The weight of the instrument will then lie on the calf of the left leg. The right leg must be bent and rest against the right side of the cello or against the edge of the back, whichever is closer.

In the *Method* of the Paris Conservatoire of 1805, one reads:

> Occasionally, the cello is rested on top of the left foot which is held in a position leaning to the left and pointing inside. The upper portion of the lower left side of the instrument is then held against the left knee; the right leg should be straight and extended forward, not held to the back—as often happens. This position, which is used by capable performers, can be convenient when playing in an orchestra as an instrument held in this way takes up less space. But it has two disadvantages: it is awkward and tires the chest since it requires one to

Figure 39. In this sketch (c. 1720) of a French abbé playing the cello, the instrument is resting directly on the floor. Pen and ink drawing by Pier Leone Ghezzi, Roman (1674–1755). *Courtesy Collection of Janos Scholz, New York.*

bend the body and lower the head when shifting down on the finger-board, and it hinders the movement of the bow because it causes it to bump into the right thigh when playing on the lower strings.

In some old illustrations, the cello can be seen resting directly on the floor (*Figure 39*), on a small stool (*Figure 40*), on a cushion (*Figure 41*), or even (albeit rarely) supported by a short stick of wood (*see Figure 12*). It was with the appearance of the great Belgian cellist François Adrien Servais (1807–1866) that a major artist used an end-pin in concert. He probably adopted the pin because his beautiful 1701 Stradivarius was a large model. Although Servais was big in stature, the dimensions of his cello made it difficult for him to hold it with his legs. Although other cellists were reluctant to follow his example, Jules Delsart, a good friend of César Franck and the first to play the cello version of this composer's celebrated Violin Sonata, finally began to require the use of the end-pin at the Paris Conservatoire in 1884.

Nicolas Platel (1777–1835), a pupil of Jean-Louis Duport and founder of the Belgian School of cello, is primarily remembered as a

Figure 40. The lady cellist stands to play, resting her instrument on a small stool. Painting, "The Music Party," by Pieter de Hooch (1632–1681).

Figure 41. This early-eighteenth-century print shows a musician standing up to play a small cello set on a cushioned stool. Engraving by Bernard Picart, French, 1701.

teacher of Servais. After only one year of study at the Brussels Conservatory, Servais was named Platel's assistant and placed in the Opera Orchestra. Although his Parisian debut as a soloist in 1834 was successful, he decided to spend two more years perfecting his art before he embarked on an extended tour in 1836. He began this tour with another concert in Paris, where he was again acclaimed, and then went on to Holland, Vienna, Prague, Warsaw, and finally Russia. In this country, blessed of cellists, he achieved a triumph. Returning again and again, he was married there in 1842. In St. Petersburg, Servais played duets with the cellist Nicolai Galitsin; and in Kiev he met Nicolai Markevitch, a pianist and amateur musician, who was a historian of the Ukraine, a close friend of the first important Russian composer, Glinka (with whom he collaborated on librettos) and my great-grandfather. Markevitch played some Ukranian melodies for Servais, who later used them in his Variations for cello.

In Leipzig in 1844, Servais took part in a concert that included the Beethoven Trio opus 97, with the famous teacher Ferdinand David playing violin and Felix Mendelssohn at the piano. That same year, with Mendelssohn on the podium, he appeared with a Berlin orchestra.

In these times, when string instrumentalists still used very little vibrato, Servais was again a pioneer in that he used it much more than his contemporaries. Inevitably, he was upbraided by some musicians for being "affected" and for making excessive use of this vibrato; but laudatory reviews of the period use the word "singing" frequently: "Servais sings at the cello." "The singing of Servais carries us to the highest spheres." "His bow sings." "His singing goes directly to the heart."

Although the king of Belgium appointed him as both solo cellist of the orchestra and teacher at the Conservatory of Brussels, where he had excellent students, he continued to tour with as much good fortune as ever. His last hectic visit to Russia took him as far as Siberia where he fell ill. Returning to his native town of Hal to rest, he died there in 1866.

Servais and Romberg were both called "Paganini of the cello," but it was the former who brought the technique of the instrument to a higher level. The size of his hands permitted him to reach the highest notes with no trouble and execute difficult passages and complex fingerings with apparent ease. One of his contemporaries wrote: "Under his large and powerful hands his cello vibrates as easily as if it were a *pochette* [a small, pocket-size violin used by dancing masters], and he has given proof of a clarity and sureness of intonation which is absolutely phenomenal." Although he left a large number of compositions for cello, as well as a Duo for violin and cello written in collaboration with Henri Vieuxtemps, only his Caprices opus 7 are remembered.

DAVID POPPER

The somewhat wild look and leonine shock of hair of David Popper (1846–1913) were very disturbing to the ladies who came to hear him play his pretty parlor pieces (*Figure 42*). One of these selections was the celebrated Gavotte in D opus 23, which he dedicated to my great-uncle Andrei Markevitch (*see Figure 26*). The composition that surely must have left them day-dreaming, however, was his Suite for

Figure 42. If David Popper's exression is any indication of his style of playing, his interpretations must have been indeed electrifying.

cello and orchestra, *Im Walde (In the Woods)* with its sections entitled "Meditation," "Autumn Flowers," and "Dance of the Gnomes."

Although Popper was born in Prague, he should be considered the founder of the Hungarian School of cello because of his classes at the Budapest Conservatory, which literally swarmed with young talent, where he taught for seventeen years. Popper himself attended the conservatory in his native Prague, studying under F. A. Kummer (1797–1879) before entering the service of the Prince of Hohenzollern at Loewenberg. Around 1863, he began to concertize throughout Germany and Austria. Winning success in Vienna, he was engaged as solo cellist of the Imperial Opera, a position he held until 1873 when he left to devote himself exclusively to a concert career. On his tours, he often played his own compositions which were well received. His Requiem for three cellos was warmly applauded at a London recital with his colleagues, the Frenchman Jules Delsart and the Englishman Edward Howell. At a concert in the famous Crystal Palace, he made a conquest with the first performance of his Concerto in C. After a concert in Vienna, however, the eminent critic Eduard Hanslick wrote the following review of Popper's performance of his own work "The Spinning Maid":

> "When the spinning wheel is portrayed musically, as in *La dame blanche* or *Der fliegende Holländer*, it is always done with a humming sound in the basses, but never—as Popper does—with a whining in the highest harmonics. When Popper gallops with the speed of a runaway horse through passages of the fastest harmonics, running chromatically from high to low and vice-versa, one soon has the impression of being in the middle of a soirée of cats on a roof and not in the melancholy chamber of a spinning maid. It is impossible to play such passages with clarity; perhaps there is a joke behind all of this—to induce in the public a new sensation blended of laughter and wonder, vacillating between the pure and the impure."

As I have already said of Casals, some of the greatest cellists did not belong to any school. Among those, I also include Luigi Boccherini, the Krafts (father and son), Bernard Romberg, and Alfredo Piatti.

LUIGI BOCCHERINI

Luigi Boccherini (1743–1805), one of the great musicians of the classical era—so great that his contemporaries put him on an equal footing with Haydn—is almost forgotten today (*Figure 43*). A prolific composer, innovative with form, he wrote an opera; about twenty symphonies; more than a hundred quintets for two violins, viola, and two cellos; nearly a hundred quartets, a form he was one of the first (like Haydn) to exploit in an elaborate manner; and a quantity of other instrumental works. But our interest in him here is as one of the greatest virtuosos of his time.

Born in Lucca, the son of a double bass player, Luigi showed an early inclination for music and a special affinity for the cello. Taking this into account, his father began giving him lessons when he was five and then sent him to study with the local maestro di cappella, who soon found himself outclassed by his pupil. At thirteen, he attracted attention playing a cello solo during a service at the Palatine Chapel, so his family decided to send him to Rome to pursue his musical studies. Arriving alone in the big city, he was soon successful in getting the well-known cellist G. B. Costanzi (1704–1778), maestro di capella at St. Peter's, to teach him cello and the basic rudiments of composition. When he was barely sixteen, he became solo cellist at the Imperial Theatre in Vienna. His father went there with him and found work as a double bass player at the Palace Chapel. He was always available to accompany Luigi whenever his son presented some of his own sonatas at the theatre, occasions on which he received much applause. It was here in Vienna that he met Gluck, who became his friend and ardent supporter.

In 1759, Boccherini and his father returned to Lucca, where Luigi was kept busy giving concerts and where he published his Six Trios opus 1. In 1765 (he was twenty-two years old), the town commissioned him to write an important cantata *La confederazione dei Sabini con Roma* for soloists, chorus, and orchestra. The following year his father died, leaving him alone and bereft of the guidance to which he was accustomed. In his distress, Luigi turned to his friend Manfredi, a well-known violinist, who was older and much more experienced.

Figure 43. This portrait of the young Luigi Boccherini (1743–1805)—the only one to show him with a cello—gives some idea of his playing position. Oil painting (c. 1764) attributed to Pompeo Batoni. *Courtesy National Gallery of Victoria, Melbourne, Australia, Everard Studley Miller Bequest, 1961. Reproduced by permission.*

They decided to join forces and try their luck abroad. After giving some concerts in northern Italy, they made their way to Paris where they had the good fortune to meet Baron de Bagge, an all-powerful figure at the Concert Spirituel. Arrangements were made for them to appear before this group at the Tuileries on March 20, 1768, and the reception both artists received was excellent. Boccherini, whose reputation as a composer had preceded him, was now acclaimed as a virtuoso as well. The *Mercure de France* said of him, "He played one of his own sonatas in a masterly fashion"; and Gluck, whom he met again in Paris, said, "The public was conquered."

After Boccherini and Manfredi had been in the French capital for a year, the Spanish ambassador offered them an opportunity to enter the service of the Prince of Asturias. They accepted and left Paris, making this comment on what they had observed there: "French artists are unbeatable in their precision and manipulation of the bow, but they are defective in their expressiveness—their instruments do not sing."

Once they arrived in Madrid, they found that the director of music at the court, Gaetano Brunetti, who dreaded the competition they would present, had schemed sufficiently well to prevent them from being engaged. Finally in 1770, after a long endeavor, Boccherini obtained the position of cellist and composer in the chamber of the Infante Don Luis, at an annual salary of thirty thousand reales, a post he would keep for fifteen years. In consequence, he could live comfortably, feel appreciated, and compose continually. He appeared in many concerts at the residence of the infante either as soloist or playing the first cello parts in his own quintets. The second cello was probably played by Don Luis, who was his pupil at the time. Although Manfredi had also obtained a position with the infante, he returned to Lucca in 1772.

During this peaceful time, Boccherini married Clementina Pelicho, a Roman, who bore him five children. An unfortunate incident during this period shows the absence of any servility in Boccherini's character. The heir to the throne, the future Charles IV, who prided himself on his violin playing, was sight-reading one of the quintets. His part contained a long passage consisting of two repeated notes and he became irritated with the monotony. "This is detestable! A beginner could do no worse," he declared. Boccherini tried vainly to make the Prince acknowledge that—with the other instruments, whose parts were interesting—his part fit into a coherent structure. Finally, in discouragement, he let fall this unfortunate remark: "My Lord, before making a valid judgment, one must be an expert!" As a result, Boccherini was immediately declared persona non grata at the royal palace, although he retained the favor of Don Luis.

From about this time on, one finds more and more allusion to Spain and its music in his writings. He even used popular folk tunes and added the guitar and castanets to his instrumentations. The Quintet G.324 opus 30, no. 6 evokes the atmosphere of the streets of Madrid at night. Favorably impressed by one of the opus 33 quartets, the Prussian ambassador suggested that he take a copy back to his country's royal heir, the future Frederick-William II, who was an amateur cellist. The prince was so enchanted with it that he thanked Boccherini most cordially and sent him a gold box as a souvenir.

Boccherini's health had been declining, and now he was suddenly plunged into despair by two disasters—the death of his wife and of his protector Don Luis. Nevertheless, Charles III appointed him first cellist of the court at a salary of 12,000 reales, and Frederick-William II named him composer of the royal chamber. Sadly enough, it seems these two men never met; the king was in Prussia and Boccherini no longer traveled outside of Spain.

The works he regularly sent to Berlin embraced all compositional forms—some quintets (a form he originated) and a quartet, "La Tirana," named after the famous Spanish actress Maria del Rosario Fernandez, known as La Tirana and immortalized by Goya in a superb portrait. This great Spanish painter met Boccherini through their admirer Don Luis. They became friends and spent much time together in Don Luis' home and in the homes of other aristocrats, mingling with many artists, painters, and writers.

Boccherini's correspondence with Haydn, which was extremely friendly, kept him up to date with the musical life of Europe. In the meantime, his music was played everywhere; and the major publishers of the day—Artaria, Pleyel, and others—vied for the honor of presenting his works.

In 1787, he married again and settled down to what he hoped would be a happy old age. He spent his time visiting with other artists, such as Romberg and the violinist Pierre Rode. When asked to become director of the newly founded Paris Conservatoire, he refused out of reluctance to leave his beloved Spain. During Lucien Bonaparte's term as French ambassador to Madrid, however, he agreed to organize some concerts "for a good price." But misfortune soon stalked him again: his health was deteriorating and spells of coughing blood came more frequently; his protector in Berlin died, and the new King Frederick-William III terminated his services—leaving him with only his meager pension from the Spanish king, which contributed little to his subsistence. Two of his daughters died in an epidemic; and two years later, his young wife and his third daughter also died. To his mental anguish was added a growing rejection on all sides and a decline of his glory. It is said that he lived with what was left of his family in a single room. In order to work in peace, he built a kind of penthouse in it, accessible only by ladder.

"The nice Boccherini," as Stendhal called him, died on 28 May 1805. In August of that year, the *Gazette Musicale Generale* of Paris said he had been "a marvelous cellist. He always charmed us with the incomparable sonority and extreme lyricism of his instrument."

I think that Boccherini's importance as a composer is seriously underestimated. He composed more than five hundred works which give dramatic evidence of a new type of construction, particularly in the innovations he made in his instrumental music. It is probable that he preceded Haydn and Mozart in writing real quartets and thereby exerted a strong influence on them. Naturally, his concertos and sonatas for cello are admirably written for the instrument. But he is perhaps so typical an example of his own epoch that his reputation could only decline after he enjoyed such great popularity during his lifetime. At a moment when opera was becoming more and more the vogue, Boccherini must have seemed a little anachronistic, but his work (though mostly unpublished) lives on and waits to be rediscovered.

ANTON KRAFT

In 1778, while Haydn was in charge of the orchestra for the Prince Esterhazy, he engaged Anton Kraft (1751–1820) as first cellist, with

Figure 44. Anton Kraft playing continuo while reading from the same score as Franz Joseph Haydn, who is playing the harpsichord. Haydn and Kraft were the only musicians at Esterhaza excused from wearing livery like that of the double bass player to the left. This watercolor (1780) shows a performance of Haydn's opera *L'Incontro improvisio. Courtesy Theater Museum, Munich.*

the understanding that Kraft would share a privilege that only Haydn enjoyed—he would not be required to wear the livery of the Prince as were the other orchestra members (*Figure 44*). A deep friendship developed between these two men to the extent that Haydn declared, "He is my son!" Haydn gave him lessons in composition, and his influence on the younger man was so great that for a long time musicologists erroneously attributed to Kraft the Concerto in D major for cello opus 101, which has all the beauty and authenticity of a Haydn work. When Prince Esterhazy died and his orchestra was disbanded in 1790, Kraft lived in Vienna under the patronage of Prince Grassalkowitz. There, he and the violinist Schuppanzigh formed a string quartet that became famous, playing under the auspices first of Prince Lichnowsky and later of Count Rasumovsky. The quartet performed mostly the works of Haydn, Mozart, and Beethoven. In fact, Kraft became very friendly with Beethoven, who said of him, "He is a poet who speaks marvelously well with his cello." Later he affectionately called him *die alte Kraft* (the old force).

From the standpoint of technique, Kraft's influence on the music of Haydn and Beethoven is very marked. One can see a change in Haydn's concertos and in the cello parts of his works (from opus 33 on) after Kraft arrived in Esterhazy. In 1789, when Kraft and Mozart were both staying at the Poland Hotel in Dresden, they spent an evening playing quartets and trios together. Mozart wrote to his wife that the performance was "very easy to listen to." As for Beethoven, one learns from some of his letters that when a work of his was performed he insisted that the cello part—which was often difficult—be assigned to Kraft. Kraft participated in the first performances of most of Beethoven's chamber works, especially the quartets. When a rivalry between Schuppanzigh and Kraft led them temporarily to form two separate quartets, Beethoven naturally took the side of his old friend; and in 1804, he composed the Triple Concerto opus 56 in his honor. Kraft also gave the first performance of Beethoven's Sonata opus 69 for cello and piano. Although Kraft's compositions, which are mostly for cello, show a strong Haydn influence, they nevertheless reveal a certain individuality.

NICOLAUS KRAFT

Nicolaus Kraft (1778–1835), son of Anton, began studying cello with his father at the age of four, using a viola because it was more in proportion with his body. By the time he was six, he had already played one of his father's compositions in concert. At eight, he accompanied the older Kraft on tour to Budapest, Dresden, and Vienna, gaining success everywhere. His father, who had studied law and philosophy at the university in his native Prague, nevertheless wanted his son to study the sciences. Only through the intervention of their new patron Prince Lobkowitz was the young Nicolaus allowed to pursue his cello studies with Duport in Berlin. He continued to give concerts in Holland, Prague, and Leipzig.

In 1809 Prince Lobkowitz offered him a life pension on the condition that Nicolaus henceforth play only in the prince's palace, never appearing elsewhere without the prince's express permission. Although Kraft agreed, the arrangement soon became burdensome—the prince's largesse in fact seriously undermined his fortune, and he fell into financial difficulties. Thus, in 1815 he was in Vienna among the artists invited to play for the dignitaries attending the Congress of Vienna. That same year, he settled in Stuttgart, where he remained for the rest of his life. He continued to give concerts, sometimes appearing with Bernhard Romberg and sometimes with one of the memorable pianists of the nineteenth century, Johann Nepomuk

Figure 45. One of the first important representatives of the German school, Bernhard Romberg (1767–1841) contributed greatly to the development of modern cello technique.

Hummel, a pupil of Mozart and a composer (he wrote a sonata for Kraft).

BERNHARD ROMBERG

The first modern virtuoso of the cello was Bernhard Romberg (1767–1841), a man whose good-natured aspect concealed a personality so acrimonious that it caused Beethoven's deplorable decision to give up the idea of writing a cello concerto (*Figure 45*).

Born at Dinklage, Oldenburg, into a family of renowned musicians, Romberg studied with his father, who was also a professional cellist. At the age of seven, he gave his first concert. He was soon touring with his cousin the violinist Andreas Romberg. Eventually they reached Paris, where the celebrated patron of the arts, Baron de Bagge, facilitated their presentation to the Concert Spirituel. Romberg was scarcely seventeen years old.

Later he became solo cellist of the Court Orchestra in Bonn while Beethoven was its first violist. At the time, Romberg got along well with Beethoven, with the violinist Franz Ries, the flutist Anton Reicha, and with Beethoven's teacher Christian Neefe, the orchestra's director. Neefe said of him: "He is an extraordinary cellist who plays his own compositions with an ardent temperament." Of one of Romberg's concerts, a music critic of the time had this to say:

> He combines in his playing an extraordinary facility with great charm. His style and expressive interpretation are perfect. He understands all the beauties of detail as well as the innate feeling of the piece. What an effect when he swells the tone to a powerful fortissimo and then follows with a diminuendo which dies out to a barely audible pianissimo.

During the French invasion in 1792, Romberg and Beethoven were forced to flee, escaping on one of the Rhine river boats and paying for their passage as kitchen boys.

In 1794, Romberg joined the orchestra of the National Theatre of Hamburg; but he soon left on a tour of Italy—again accompanied by his cousin. Returning by way of Vienna, he got an opportunity to appear in concert, through Beethoven's recommendation. There he also met Haydn, who was impressed with his talent. Engagements to play took him to London, Spain, and Portugal. In fact, during a gala soirée at the Lisbon Court, King Ferdinand VII himself accompanied him. Going on to Paris, he spent two years giving a series of triumphal concerts and was subsequently named a professor at the Paris Conservatoire. By 1805, he was back in Berlin as solo cellist of the Royal Chapel, but his relationship with the Duport brothers, who had been in residence there for a long time, was extremely unfriendly. Within a year, Romberg was again on the road, first to Vienna and then on his initial visit to Russia. While playing in the Ukraine and other southern areas, he heard some folk melodies that he later used in some of his compositions. He was preparing to go to Moscow when the invading French again upset his plans, leading him to go to Scandinavia instead. Thereafter, Hamburg became his home base for the rest of his life, but he made still another tour across Europe, and in 1813 he went again to Russia, where he stayed for two years. Everywhere he went, he met with great success: in Milan he was nicknamed "the Paganini of the cello"; and in Leipzig a critic wrote, "No other artist, since Mozart, excites me with his playing and his writing as does Romberg." Other cellists who tried to emulate him—such as Max Bohrer (1783–1867)—encountered commentaries of this type:

"Romberg plays for eternity and Bohrer plays for the salons." Through his extensive traveling, he became widely known; and at the same time, his compositions also gained great popularity.

Before Romberg's career, a musician was content to make a living in one place, playing in a private orchestra or in a royal chapel, giving only a few isolated concerts here and there. Romberg, whose lifestyle was just the opposite, was able to bring back reflections on what he had observed, such as the following:

> An allegro is played more rapidly in Paris than in Vienna, and more quickly in Vienna than in the north of Germany. Consequently, I cannot tell you at what tempo a particular movement should be executed because there is not one composer who will play, at the same rate of speed, all those movements in his compositions for which he has indicated the same tempo.

This is a valid explanation on the subjective aspect of interpretation which deals with tempi.

Romberg was much loved in Russia. He made frequent visits there and had many friends, one in particular being the amateur cellist Mathieu Vielgorsky, who always welcomed him with open arms. In addition, one of the first good Russian luthiers, Ivan Batov (1767–1841), showed his regard by making him a cello. Although Romberg owned a magnificent Stradivarius from 1711, he liked the new instrument very much. He was interested in the folklore of the country, and among his numerous compositions we find some that were obviously inspired by it: Russian Air with Variations opus 14, opus 19 and opus 52; Two Variations on Two Russian Melodies opus 20; Caprice on Russian Songs opus 38; and Souvenir of St. Petersburg opus 77, a fantasy based on themes from the pen of Michel Vielgorsky. As was the case elsewhere, his influence on the Russian School of cello was enormous, and he had a great many pupils. Later on, however, he published a rather disappointing method in which he recommended certain laughable procedures, such as holding a cork in the palm of the left hand while playing.

Stendhal said of him: "With what pleasurable delight we should be drawn to the cellist Romberg if, instead of having a soul which is honest and without the faults of the bourgeois, he had, excitingly, that of a Werther." Surprising as it seems considering his apparent popularity, Romberg had frequent attacks of bad humor, and his relationships with the other musicians were rather bitter. This man who was called "the king of all the virtuosi," the "cellists' hero" said of his talented young colleagues Dotzauer and Kummer: "with brains like coffee beans, there is nothing for them but to go to school and study." He had the same attitude toward Beethoven who, possessed of a difficult personality himself, nevertheless had only sympathy and admiration for him. In his autobiography, the great German violinist Ludwig Spohr observes that Romberg was astonished that Spohr could bring himself to play "something as absurd" as Beethoven's Quartets opus 18. He also said that this same composer's Quartet in F opus 59 the "Rasumovsky," was an "infamous hoax." It is not surprising to learn that when Beethoven offered to write a concerto for Romberg, he ungraciously said that he would never study it and that he never played anything but his own compositions. It is because of such a blind reaction on the part of this egocentric—who was able neither to recognize the genius of Beethoven nor to appreciate a good friend—that we must consign this project to the column of "lost" concertos.

The list of Romberg's works is long; but except for a few cello pieces still played in conservatories, all of them are forgotten today. Unwisely, he tried to prolong his career for too many years, and he received this of his last concert in Paris: "It was a sad spectacle to see an old man who does not wish to give up something of which he is no longer capable, and who seems to take pleasure in dealing mortal blows to his good reputation."

ALFREDO PIATTI

It is interesting to note how many important cellists began studying the instrument with their fathers. The famous Italian Alfredo Piatti (1822–1901) did not deviate from this rule (*Figure 46*). Born in Bergamo, he studied with his father and then with his great-uncle before he entered the Milan Conservatory in the class of the well-known teacher Vincenzo Merighi. At fifteen years of age, after a successful debut at La Scala, he immediately began touring Europe,

Figure 46. This photograph taken at the end of the nineteenth century shows that Alfredo Piatti (1822–1901), whose virtuosity was legendary, was still not using an end-pin.

continuing to win acclaim from all sides. In Vienna, he was described as "incomparable" by the celebrated and formidable critic Eduard Hanslick. In 1843, he was invited to perform in Munich, where his playing so impressed Franz Liszt that he presented the young Italian with a superb Amati cello and encouraged him to make appearances in Paris and London. Eventually, he spent the greater part of his life in the English capital. At a concert there directed by Mendelssohn, the composer-conductor was so enchanted he declared, "I must write a concerto for Piatti," and immediately began work on it. When it was finished, he dedicated it to Piatti and sent it to him by mail, but it never reached its destination—one more masterwork to be registered in the catalogue of "lost" concertos.

In 1845, on the recommendation of the Russian cellist Vielgorsky, Piatti made his debut in Russia. The critics were unanimous in emphasizing "the extent of his technique, his huge and beautiful sonority, his exemplary clarity, his impeccable taste, his expression and the seduction of his lyricism." Throughout his long career, the public remained sensitive to his charm and his style. One can still get an idea of his refinement from his editions of old cello works. His realizations are so far superior to other publications of the day that there is no comparison. Most of the others were characterized by flagrant bad taste.

Piatti was greatly valued by other musicians for his splendid performances of chamber music. With Joseph Joachim, the renowned violinist, he organized concerts in London that proved very popular. During these, if a violist were lacking, he never hesitated to play the viola part in a quartet, holding the instrument between his knees like a cello. The audiences for the London pops concerts idolized him.

During a tour of Ireland, he discovered an outstanding Stradivarius from 1720, which he acquired and played exclusively until his death in 1901. He was an active composer; but apart from his Twelve Caprices opus 25, his works for cello are completely forgotten.

LISA CRISTIANI

For a long time, the cello was considered the exclusive appanage of the male sex. Because it was difficult to play in a side-saddle position, women had to wait until the end-pin had come into general use before they could apply themselves seriously to the study of this instrument. One of the first women to make a name for herself as a cellist was Lisa Cristiani (1827–1853), a Parisian who caught Mendelssohn's attention at one of her concerts in Leipzig in 1845 (*Figure* 47). Succumbing to the charm of this pretty eighteen-year-old artist, he wrote his ravishing Song without Words opus 109 for her. Playing her 1700 Stradivarius, she toured Europe, garnering constant commendation for her gracious playing. Eventually, she went to Russia where she traveled extensively, giving concerts from St. Petersburg to Tiflis. In Kiev in 1852, at the home of Nicolai Markevitch she met Servais; and these three musicians spent many evenings playing chamber music together. Cristiani and Servais both being very popular, the inevitable comparisons were made, including this: "If one listens to the Belgian

Figure 47. This pretty cellist, Lisa Christiani (1827–1853) toured extensively, although she lived to be only twenty-six.

cellist, one pricks up one's ears, but with the petite Frenchwoman one listens with the heart." On what turned out to be her last tour, she made the difficult journey across Siberia to Kamtchatka. On the way back, she stopped to give a recital at Tobolsk, a small village on the steppes, where she was received with the usual warm applause. Shortly thereafter, she contracted cholera, and she died in Novocherkask. She was only twenty-six years old. Her treasured cello found its way into the hands of Hugo Becker.

In our day, the number of noteworthy female cellists has increased markedly; but until the latter part of this century, only two achieved fame—Guilhermina Suggia and Beatrice Harrison.

GUILHERMINA SUGGIA

Guilhermina Suggia (1888–1950), who was later to become Casals's first wife, was born in Oporto, Portugal (*Figure 48*). She studied in Leipzig with Julius Klengel, who stated, "I am the greatest admirer

Figure 48. The famous and marvelous portrait of Guilhermina Suggia in 1923 by the noted English painter Augustus John. *Courtesy the Tate Gallery, London.*

of her phenomenal talent." In tribute, his Caprice in the form of a Chaconne opus 43, a highly virtuoso piece for solo cello, is dedicated to her. With the illustrious Artur Nikisch conducting, she made her debut in 1905 at a Gewandhaus concert. In London in the same year, she had tremendous success with the Dvořák concerto, still a relatively new work, having been composed in 1895. The public was captivated both by her remarkable technique and by the sonority of her tone, which had a powerful masculine quality rarely heard from a female cellist. A little while later, she became a pupil of Casals, an association that led to marriage and a career devoted solely to joint concerts with her celebrated husband. The marriage lasted only six years, however, and after the divorce, she resumed her own career, concentrating her activities in England and Portugal.

BEATRICE HARRISON

The inimitable English cellist Beatrice Harrison (1892–1965) began life in Roorker, India—then part of the British Empire—but was taken to England at an early age. In London, she studied with William Whitehouse (1859–1935) who had been a favored pupil of Piatti. Although by the time she was fourteen she had already played in Queen's Hall, she went on to further study with Hugo Becker at the Berlin Hochschule. Her debut in that city in 1910 led to a series of engagements across Europe. On her return to London, she appeared with the well-known pianist and composer Eugen d'Albert (1864–1932), a former pupil of Liszt. From this moment on, her reputation grew steadily, especially in England and the Anglophile countries. She was a great protagonist of modern music and inspired some excellent works for cello. In her honor Frederick Delius (1862–1934) composed a sonata, a cello concerto, and a concerto for violin and cello, which she played with her sister May, who was an accomplished violinist. The Cello Concerto written in 1919 by Sir Edward Elgar (1857–1934) was one of her favorites. She was also one of the very few cellists to play the Kodály Sonata opus 8 for solo cello during the 1920s.

KARL DAVIDOV

In Russia at the beginning of the nineteenth century, there were some excellent amateur cellists like Galitsin and Vielgorsky; but the Russian School properly speaking began with Karl Davidov (1838–1889), the first great professional cellist (*Figure 49*). His exceptional artistic and pedagogic gifts gave vigor to a conception of cello playing that continues successfully today.

The son of a successful physician who was also an amateur violinist, Davidov grew up in Moscow in an intellectual environment. His father's home was a meeting place for artists who enjoyed attending

Figure 49. Karl Davidov (1838–1889) founded the Russian school. Tchaikovsky described him as the "Tsar of violoncellists."

the musical soirées that were frequent occurrences there. Early in his life, Karl began the study of the piano; he then went on to the cello, taking lessons with André Schmidt (1810–1862), a Czech who was first cellist of the Bolshoi Theatre Orchestra. At the age of nine, he played in a concert of chamber music; and at fourteen he made his debut at the Bolshoi, playing a difficult bravura piece by the eminent German cellist Max Bohrer. Of this debut, a critic wrote, "We have heard this young virtuoso with rapture." Davidov then decided to study with Karl Schuberth in order to perfect skills.

Karl Schuberth (1811–1863), who had been a pupil of Dotzauer, possessed, in addition to a talent for the cello, certain gifts for composition, conducting, and organizing. From his twentieth year on, he concertized across Europe—performing in Germany, Belgium, Holland, and England and making a successful appearance in Paris in 1834. It was in Russia, however, that he won the most acclaim. Upon being invited to give some courses at the University of St. Petersburg, he became a permanent resident of that country. He founded a student orchestra, directed the orchestra of the St. Petersburg Theatre, and when a conservatory was established in that city, obtained a post as professor. He also composed a large number of works, one of which is entitled "Polyhymnia, Concerto Patetico." At a concert given in his honor during the last year of his life, he shared the podium with Richard Wagner, conducting an orchestra of 150 musicians who had been gathered for the occasion.

In studying with Schuberth, Davidov thus fell heir to the great tradition of Duport, which had come to Schuberth through Kriegck and Dotzauer. While studying with Schuberth, Davidov also composed two operas, *Les Mineurs* and *Caligula*. Then at the age of seventeen, he embarked on four years at the university as a student of physics and mathematics. During all the time he was a student, he maintained an excellent academic standing, even though he continued with his music and gave an increasing number of concerts—with continuously growing success. In addition, his compositions were being performed; in 1858, his Fantasie for four cellos and bass on themes from his opera *Caligula* received a performance in which Davidov himself played the first cello part. One critic predicted a brilliant future for him, adding later:

> We have already taken note of his exceptional gifts, but no one could have anticipated so much progress in so little time. In the past year the concerts of M. Servais have left a definite imprint on Davidov, many of the remarkable qualities of the great Belgian have been assimilated by the young artist. The public awarded him a dazzling success which was richly deserved.

Servais himself, greatly impressed by Davidov's talent, predicted that the young musician would attain great glory.

Finishing his studies at the university, Davidov went to Leipzig where he enrolled in a class in music theory at the conservatory (which Tchaikovsky called at that time the most conservative of conservatories) where one of his classmates was Edvard Grieg (1843–1907). Opportunity knocked, as it were, when Friedrich Grützmacher, who was scheduled to play a Mendelssohn trio with pianist Ignaz Moscheles and violinist Ferdinand David, suddenly became too ill to fill the engagement. Davidov substituted for him on the spot and made such a tremendous impression he was offered the position as first cellist with the celebrated Gewandhaus Orchestra. With this group, in 1859, he played his First Concerto opus 5. The conductor was Julius

Rietz, also a cellist and composer, and the occasion was an enormous success. Davidov was admired for his impeccable technique, for the mathematical precision of his intonation, for the manner in which he made his instrument sing, and the musicality and taste of his composition. This performance immediately placed him among the leading cellists of the day. He continued to perform throughout Germany and played in Paris and London in 1860—always with acclaim. Meanwhile, he acquired an Amati cello. He also agreed to replace Grützmacher as professor at the Leipzig Conservatory. In his class there, one of the pupils was the brother of his former classmate, Grieg. After two years at the conservatory, however, he decided to return to Russia. When he left Germany, he was known there as "the foremost and best-loved of all cellists."

On his return to his native land, he gave a concert at the Bolshoi in Moscow, winning the following commentary: "We have regained not a richly endowed musician, but a colossal talent, one who is no longer a Muscovite artist but a European celebrity, a cellist who has no rival at the present time." He accepted an offer from Anton Rubinstein to teach the cello class at the newly founded conservatory in St. Petersburg, where he also gave some courses in the history of music, the first of their kind in Russia. Some of Davidov's many students who are worthy of mention include Alexander Viergebilovitch (1849–1911), who gained much recognition during the last twenty years of the nineteenth century; Alfred von Glehn; Hanus Wihan (1855–1920), the foremost Czech cellist and professor at the Prague Conservatory; Julius Klengel, noted professor at the Leipzig Conservatory; Karl Fuchs (1865–1951), a professor at the Royal College of Music in London; and the celebrated English cellist Leo Stern (1862–1904). Davidov demanded a great deal from his students. He was in the habit of saying that—since it is a known fact that one loses 50 percent of one's resources when playing in concert—in order to have the 100 percent capability desired, it is essential to have a 200 percent knowledge of the composition.

Davidov's artistry won for him another kind of accolade—the gift of a lovely Stradivarius cello. Its owner, the esteemed and venerable cellist Mathieu Vielgorsky, was so impressed by the majestic way in which Davidov played a Romberg concerto that sometime during the year before his death he decided to give the instrument to the younger man. Choosing one of Davidov's concerts as the occasion to make the presentation, he waited until the end. Then, in the presence of the astonished audience, he gave the instrument to Davidov with these words: "I have found no one more deserving to receive my Stradivarius than you."

In 1869, Davidov gave the Schumann Concerto its Russian premiere with the composer and conductor Mili Balakirev on the podium. The enthusiastic audience included Borodin and Rimsky-Korsakov. This work was a special favorite of Davidov's and he programmed it frequently. In 1871, after one performance, another Russian composer, César Cui (son of a French officer who had remained in Moscow after the retreat from Russia in 1812) reported that in his fingers the Schumann was "elegant, beautiful, musical, and very interesting from the first note to the last."

By this time, Davidov's schedule had become almost superhuman. In addition to teaching and performing as a soloist, he took part in many chamber music concerts, conducted the symphonic concerts of the Russian Musical Society of St. Petersburg, and served as cellist in this organization's quartet. The first violinist in this group was the celebrated Leopold Auer—teacher of Jascha Heifetz, Mischa Elman, Efrem Zimbalist, Nathan Milstein, and many others. Davidov played trios with Anton Rubinstein and Henri Wieniawski and sonatas with Saint-Saëns and Liszt. The pianist and conductor Hans von Bülow (1830–1894), often played Davidov's piano accompaniments, although he refused to do the same for anybody else. Moreover he declared, "It goes without saying; superlatives to Davidov!"

In addition, Davidov played all over Europe, garnering immense success and laudatory reviews wherever he went. In Cologne they said "all virtuosi should be guided by him"; in Berlin, "no cellist has ever given us so much pleasure"; in Frankfurt, "incomparable—the playing of an inspired master"; in Paris, from a review in *Le Siècle* in 1875, after an appearance at the Pasdeloup Concerts, "one of the most remarkable cellists we have ever heard." The teacher Hugo Becker named him "he who has wakened the comprehension of the musical aesthetic in the realm of cello playing." Tchaikovsky's description is perhaps both the shortest and the finest: "Tsar of violoncellists!"

Figure 50. Leopold Rostropovitch (1892–1942), father of Mstislav.

LEOPOLD ROSTROPOVITCH

At the time, Parisian newspaper critics offered comments such as these:

> Rostropovitch aroused the enthusiasm of the listeners with the security of his technique and with the character and temperament of his interpretation.

> The cello playing of the young Russian artist M. Rostropovitch afforded us an evening full of pleasant discoveries. He displayed a remarkable technique and a very significant originality of expression; his phrasing was always pure and admirable. With certainty we can anticipate for Mr. Rostropovitch, who is only eighteen years old, a brilliant future.

These lines, written in 1911, refer to Leopold Rostropovitch (1892–1942), the father of Mstislav (*Figure* 50). He was born at Voronege, into a family of musicians, and took his first musical steps with his father. At a very early age, although studying the piano, he began to show great propensity for the cello. By the age of twelve, he had realized these exceptional musical gifts and was already playing in public. He continued his studies with Alexander Viergebilovitch, a teacher at the St. Petersburg Conservatory, a disciple of Davidov, and one of the best representatives of his school. When he was fifteen, Rostropovitch began to teach cello in a private music school.

Rostropovitch's personality and behavior as a student at the conservatory gave rise to conflicting opinions. From one of his classmates came the story that "often the young, disorderly, overexcited and talented Rostropovitch came into class like a storm, opening the door with a bang. He would throw himself around Viergebilovitch's neck and then demonstrate for him a passage from any unexpected concerto whatsoever; or more likely, he would hurl himself at the piano and accompany one of us 'on the spot.'" Viergebilovitch himself said of him, "full of talent, what a loss that he cuts classes and may accomplish nothing." But from the celebrated composer Glazunov, the director of the conservatory, came this evaluation, "a beautiful tone and extremely talented phrasing . . . a flawless, natural technique . . . ideal hands," and later, "a great virtuoso and musical talent."

At his first big concert, which took place in Warsaw in 1911 with the Philharmonic Orchestra, his interpretation of the Böellmann Symphonic Variations was warmly received, and the critics were enthusiastic. Soon thereafter, he went to Paris where he took lessons from Pablo Casals, who always remembered him well as a student. From then on, he divided his time between teaching in several conservatories and making concert tours across Russia. Everywhere he went, he impressed audiences with his artistic temperament, his beautiful and powerful singing tone, and his facile technique. He was also known as a composer of works for the piano and for the cello; among the latter were four concertos and a Classical Suite for solo cello. It is only natural that his own son Mstislav was among his best students.

Although weakened by illness, Rostropovitch nevertheless continued his activities, giving countless recitals in hospitals for the wounded of World War II. At his last concert, in April of 1942, he introduced a concerto written by his son, who accompanied him at the piano. Like his father, Mstislav is a gifted pianist as well as a cellist and is becoming increasingly well known as a conductor.

Figure 51. Gregor Piatigorsky (1903–1976) in a photograph taken in 1975.

GREGOR PIATIGORSKY

At the age of seven, I had my first encounter with Gregor Piatigorsky (1903–1976), one of the most important cellists in our history (*Figure 51*). On my half-size cello, I played the first movement of Popper's Concerto opus 24 (*Figure 52*). My performance must have been sufficiently acceptable because when I had finished he asked me to repeat the piece for his wife Lyda (divorced later, she married the French cellist Pierre Fournier). On this day, which was so memorable for me, I was struck with the sweet expression, the extreme kindness, and the aristocratic manner of this good-natured giant who was to become my master a few years later.

Piatigorsky's crowded and romantic life began in the Russian village of Iekaterinoslav, now known as Dniepropetrovsk. This city was founded in 1787 by Potemkin—to the glory of Catherine II. It is

Figure 52. Dimitry Markevitch as a child in a pen and ink drawing by Jean Cocteau (1889–1963), the multifaceted French genius.

situated in southern Ukraine, on the bank of the Dnieper, in one of the richest agricultural regions of the world. Its vast steppes, with the famous "black earth" area, were the scene of marvelous escapades for the small Grisha. Those endless horizons must surely have had a determining influence on him, one reflected in his great breadth of spirit and outlook on life.

When Gregor was just seven, his father, an unsuccessful violinist employed in the family bookstore, found him playing on a pretend cello he had made from two sticks of wood. The elder Piatigorsky immediately bought him his first instrument and gave him some lessons; but the paternal pedagogy left much to be desired, and Gregor was soon entrusted to a real teacher at the local conservatory. One day he was made to play an audition for a certain Monsieur Kinkoulkine, a pupil of the great teacher Julius Klengel. When asked his opinion, his verdict fell like a knife: "Give up the cello, you have no talent at all."

Gregor nursed his chagrin for a week and then resumed his lessons with even more determination. Meanwhile, his father decided to continue his own musical studies; and leaving his family without support, he went to Moscow to work with the great violinist Leopold Auer. Although only eight, Grisha found work in a nightclub, but he was discharged shortly because his youthful presence inhibited the customers in their pursuit of pleasure. He next found employment in a movie house, where he had great fun watching the films. At this time, when his grandfather died, his father returned to claim his inheritance and remove the entire family to Moscow. This was a fateful move for Grisha—it permitted him, at the age of nine, to enter the Moscow Conservatory, where he would study with a Davidov pupil, Alfred von Glehn (1858–1927). His father's careless management quickly wiped out the money from the legacy, so Grisha went back to work—in orchestras of second-rate opera houses or in spots like the Café Chantant where he was positioned with his back to the stage so that he could not see the scantily clad women on display there. He was not a good student, and the worthy von Glehn was not a demanding teacher—he preferred to spend his time practicing alone and composing for the cello—but Grisha nevertheless passed his examinations brilliantly. He continued to play in cafés, with some unusual results. One night, irritated because he played some Bach, a drunken customer broke his cello. Later on, however, when he was playing at one of the best restaurants in Moscow, an unknown amateur (who was a steady customer) presented him with a cello worth nine thousand rubles—a pretty sum!

Another evening, while Grisha was playing at the fashionable Metropole Restaurant, he noticed Alexander Glazunov among the diners. In his honor, Grisha played the composer's lovely "Chant du Menestrel" and "Serenade Espagnole." Glazunov was touched and entertained the young cellist at his table, lavishing encouragement and fatherly advice on him—as well as food.

When the famous basso Feodor Chaliapin (*see Figure* 56) was looking for a musician to entertain audiences while he rested between groups of songs, he engaged Piatigorsky but shortly thereafter dismissed him. The huge success with which he was received did not please the celebrated singer.

At the time of the Revolution, when Piatigorsky was fourteen, he was engaged by a serious quartet as a replacement for the excellent cellist Vassily Podgorny. At first the group was known as the Lenin Quartet, but later it became the First State Quartet. On one occasion, they were invited to perform at the Kremlin. After tea had been served, they played a movement from a Grieg quartet for an audience of one—Lenin.

Before he was fifteen, Grisha applied for—and readily obtained—the position of first cello in the orchestra of the Bolshoi Theatre. He was also playing chamber music in a number of concerts—quartets, trios, and sonatas. With the composer, he gave the first reading of Prokofiev's Ballade opus 15; and he introduced to Russia the Debussy Sonata, the Ravel Trio, and *Don Quixote* of Richard Strauss. The new government drafted him to play in the factories and in clubs set up both for the Red Army and for the workers. He was paid "in kind," and his ration card—unlike those of the other members of the Bolshoi Orchestra—was that of a child. Because it entitled him to additional sweets, his colleagues nicknamed him *Chocolate Baby*.

In 1921, recognizing the need to expand his horizons and wanting to study in Germany, he applied for permission to leave Russia. He was refused. He then made up his mind to escape; and taking advantage of a concert engagement in a city near the Polish border, he crossed the frontier by swimming a river, holding his cello on top of his head. After many adventures and misadventures, he reached Warsaw where he obtained a chair in the Philharmonic Orchestra. He was well liked there, despite a thoughtless practical joke he played on one of his elderly colleagues. He tied a rope to this man's cello; the other end of the rope was attached in the flyspace above the stage. During a change of scene, then, a cello suddenly and slowly rose into the air, finally disappearing in the upper reaches above the stage. Grisha adored practical jokes of this kind. All his life, he loved to make people laugh.

A generous American on a mission in Poland was impressed by his talent. Learning that it was Piatigorsky's objective to study in Germany, he offered to pay all his traveling expenses to Berlin and to support him completely while he studied there. At last, at the age of nineteen, he could finally live without constantly worrying about the next day.

When he arrived in the German capital, he joined the class of the celebrated but severe Hugo Becker, a disciple of Grützmacher. Becker insisted that Grisha forget everything he knew and begin again from the beginning. Becker was the only teacher who ever made him pay for his lessons; and he roused only antipathy in Piatigorsky, who did not appreciate his sarcasm. At the end of his fifth lesson, in response to Becker's statement that the lesson was finished, Piatigorsky inadvertently—through his limited knowledge of German—said "Gott sei Dank (thank God)" and was expelled at once. He then went to Leipzig to study with Julius Klengel in whom he found an affable, congenial teacher—the eternal cigar in his mouth yellowing his white beard. Klengel's pupils, who came from all over, adored him and developed among themselves an atmosphere of mutual aid and close friendship. Klengel's pedagogical skills consisted essentially of encouraging speeches and the advice that his pupils always listen carefully to one another. His solicitude for others even went so far as to help Grisha in rescuing a poor prostitute who had been evicted from her home.

After a bitter dispute with his American benefactor, Piatigorsky returned to Berlin. Without funds and without work, he was obliged to sleep on a bench in the Tiergarten. He soon found a job playing at the Café Ruscho, a gathering place for artists, actors, and musicians—among whom was Emanuel Feuermann, who came there regularly for coffee. This job was followed by an engagement with a professional trio, the Pozniak, which traveled all over Germany. Meanwhile, he seized several opportunities to give recitals, which were always well received.

One day—forced to flee precipitously from the arms of a beautiful countess in order to avoid the wrath of her jealous husband—he found himself once more on a bench in the Tiergarten. By a lucky chance, one of his old friends saw him there and told him that a cellist was being sought to play a new work although the job would be without pay. Since he was unemployed anyway, Piatigorsky accepted. The year was 1923 and the occasion was a performance of Arnold Schoenberg's *Pierrot Lunaire*. Artur Schnabel was the pianist and Fritz Stiedry, the conductor, coordinated the parts of the narrator and five musicians that this work comprises. During the three weeks of rehearsals, Grisha lived on sandwiches, provided by Schnabel during the rest periods. The performance was a great success.

Shortly thereafter, this same friend told him he had spoken about him to the conductor of the Berlin Philharmonic, Wilhelm Furtwängler, who wanted to hear him play. For his audition, Piatigorsky played movements from several of the big concertos, as well as passages from orchestral scores. Furtwängler was conquered and immediately offered the position of first cello in his orchestra to this young man, who was barely twenty-one years old. A little later, he signed a contract with one of the most important impresarios in Germany and began to get bookings in other countries. In France, he played all the sonatas and variations of Beethoven with Furtwängler at the piano. At the end of one concert, Maurice Ravel said to him: "You play admirably well, but why do you perform such bad music?"

"But it is Beethoven."

"That's right, that is what I said," responded Ravel.

Solo engagements became more and more numerous; and after four years, he was forced to resign from the orchestra. With Schnabel and Carl Flesch he organized a trio that rapidly became celebrated throughout Europe. His partners had only one fault to find: Piatigorsky was constantly forgetting his music. One day, they put the part from a Wagner opera on his music stand instead of the part for the Schubert trio on the program. The moment he attacked the first note, Grisha saw the substitution. After a momentary hesitation, he imperturbably played the Schubert part from memory, to the extent of turning the pages at the required places. Schnabel and Flesch were convulsed with laughter and had trouble concealing their mirth from the audience. It was a spirited performance.

In the course of his travels, he met the great scientist Albert Einstein, who was an amateur violinist of very mediocre quality. After subjecting Grisha to some painful scratching, he asked how he had played. Piatigorsky extricated himself brilliantly by replying: "Relatively well."

By this time, Vladimir Horowitz and Nathan Milstein had also left Russia. The three joined forces and placed themselves under the management of a man—a genius in his field—who booked them throughout the world, both individually and as a trio. The success of these superb artists, who had come to be called the "Three Musketeers," was phenomenal.

In 1929, Piatigorsky made his first tour of the United States. It began with a recital at the Oberlin Conservatory and a concert with the Philadelphia Orchestra under Leopold Stokowsky. His reception was triumphant, and engagements followed with increasing rapidity until he was soon playing everywhere and under the best conductors—Mengelberg, Toscanini, Mitropoulos, and others. One highlight for him was the concert in which he played *Don Quixote* under the direction of Strauss himself. When it was over, Strauss told him, "I have finally heard my *Don Quixote* as I conceived it."

In London, under the auspices of His Master's Voice RCA Victor, he recorded the Schumann concerto with the London Philharmonic, John Barbirolli—himself a cellist—conducting. This recording, which is out of press and brings an insane price in the collectors' market, was an incredible success for more than one reason. First, it was done with extreme artistry, representing one of the great moments in recorded cello music—the tone is superb, the style and phrasing marvelous, and the technique impeccable. Although cut at 78 RPM and without modern fidelity, it always gives me the same pleasure when I hear it. Second, it marks a significant date in recording history—it was one of the first times that a concerto (and one for cello at that) was recorded nonstop. The usual procedure at the time was to break a composition into four-minute segments, the duration of a playing side. In order to cut this recording without a pause, the sound engineers used two turntables in relay so as to eliminate all breaks. Finally, accomplishing this tour de force, including the rehearsal with orchestra, took only forty minutes.

During one of his many tours of the United States, his accompanist fell ill. Someone recommended a replacement, a piano teacher at the university in the city where he was to give his next recital. Arriving two days early, Piatigorsky went to the home of his substitute accompanist for a rehearsal and found a charming man—in wonderfully comfortable surroundings. Installed in a deep armchair with a drink in his hand, he and his host conversed at length on a variety of subjects before getting down to the business of the next day's program. It seemed that the pianist had already played all the numbers and knew them perfectly, so they agreed to postpone their rehearsal until the next day. Piatigorsky was thoroughly delighted to have the opportunity—for once—to rest. After a good night's sleep, he returned to the pianist's house where he was given some delicious coffee. Then he suggested that they go through the program once, at any rate. The moment they began the Debussy Sonata, however, Grisha saw the pianist literally go to pieces. He demanded to know what was wrong and learned—to his stupefaction—that the man did not know how to play: he had been teaching for twenty years without being able to play one note on the piano. Practically in tears, he threw himself at Piatigorsky's feet and begged him not to reveal his secret. He suggested that they could claim the music for the program had been lost and that the artist had decided to give a recital of works for solo cello. Grisha agreed to this—to the good fortune of the audience, who made it a triumph for him. Who knows? Perhaps that man is still out there, still respected by all.

A recital of an entirely different type was the one he gave in Budapest with Béla Bartók, playing the First Rhapsody with the great Hungarian composer at the piano. Piatigorsky's amiable relations with many modern composers gave rise to a number of interesting works: concertos by Prokofiev, Walton, Hindemith, Dukelsky, Castelnuovo-Tedesco, and others. He collaborated with Igor Stravinsky on the Suite Italienne for cello and piano, which is based on themes from the same composer's *Pulcinella*. There is an interesting story about this collaboration. Stravinsky generously insisted that Piatigorsky accept half the royalties, but as it turned out when the accounts were settled, he—as composer—kept 90 percent, and the amount divided in half was the 10 percent reserved for the arrangers, leaving only 5 percent for poor Grisha.

In 1938, he discovered an unpublished manuscript of an Intermezzo for cello and piano by Claude Debussy in a second-hand music shop in Paris. He made this work available to cellists by publishing it in America during the war. It was also through him that Anton Webern's compositions were introduced to the public at a time when the composer was totally unknown. On 3 June 1970 at the Cleveland Institute of Music, with the pianist Victor Babin, he also gave the first performances of an extant sonata movement (1914) and Two Pieces

Figure 53. "Violoncelle" was a racehorse belonging to Baron Guy de Rothschild, named in honor of Gregor Piatigorsky, the baron's brother-in-law.

(1899) by Webern. These works were discovered in 1965 in the attic of the Webern family home in Perchtoldsdorf, Austria. In a 1926 recital in Berlin he had already played the Three Little Pieces opus 11. On the lighter side was the collection of short pieces he used as encores and which he called his "insects"—"The Bee" of Schubert, "The Mosquito" of Fairchild, "The Flight of the Bumblebee" of Rimsky-Korsakov and "The Butterfly" of Fauré. He had many occasions to use these (*Figure 53*).

In 1961, he and Jascha Heifetz founded the Heifetz-Piatigorsky Concerts, which were dedicated to chamber music. The artists played mainly in California or in New York at Carnegie Hall. Luckily for us, they made many admirable recordings, inviting such artists as the violist William Primrose to join them. When they appeared with Artur Rubinstein, the American press called them the "Million Dollar Trio."

Along with all this playing—for which he used two superb instruments, both by Stradivari, acquired in rapid succession, the "Baudiot" of 1725 and the "Batta" of 1714—he did a considerable amount of teaching: from 1942 to 1951, he taught cello at the Curtis Institute, which was directed at that time by the violinist Efrem Zimbalist. During the summers, he directed chamber music classes at Tanglewood, a summer festival established in the Berkshires by Serge Koussevitzky, conductor of the Boston Symphony Orchestra; and from 1961 until his death, he gave courses at the University of Southern California in Los Angeles.

Referring to teaching, Piatigorsky said "One who teaches should be one who gives"; and he was strongly interested in working with young musicians and in helping with their lives and problems. To encourage and stimulate them, he established a prize which is awarded regularly. The French cellist Guy Fallot was the first recipient. His associations with his pupils were always cordial—even affectionate—but they were never allowed to lapse into familiarity. He was wont to say, "I have never had pupils, only friends." I remember so vividly the atmosphere that pervaded his home near Hollywood where he and his wife Jacqueline entertained so pleasingly. But music was always foremost. I would scarcely arrive before he said to me, "Play something for me." To the very end of our relationship, his comments and wise counsel always supported me in my work. His maxim was "Study—study—always study, because we are perpetual students. Our struggle for better knowledge brings us neither medals nor honor, only joy. This is why musicians are happy—they live with beauty, which is always pleasant but never easy."

He always found just the right words to encourage the young people who came to him. On one occasion, a girl from Holland, who had long wanted to study with him, appeared at his home in California without any warning. Piatigorsky let her play for him; but after a few notes, he could tell she had no talent at all. Nevertheless he gave her a lesson on one note—a C—explaining fully the means of producing a pleasant tone and good intonation. Finally, after a great deal of effort, she succeeded in showing a bit of improvement; and he sent her away with these words, "You must do the same thing with the D and E and so on, until you have worked like this on every note of the cello. Then you will be a good cellist."

He had a great aversion for the many bad editions one encounters everywhere of the great classical compositions for cello. In 1975, he visited a class at the Institute for Advanced Musical Studies, which I founded in Montreux, Switzerland (*Figure* 54). When a student played the Haydn D major Concerto in the Gevaert edition, I heard him say, "The best thing that you can do with this edition is make a present of it to your worst enemy" (*Figure* 55).

Figure 54. Gregor Piatigorsky and the author in 1975 conducting a master class at the Institute for Advanced Musical Studies in Montreux, Switzerland.

Figure 55. The author and Piatigorsky playing cello duets for a student audience.

Piatigorsky was blessed with a remarkable physique. When he walked on stage holding his cello at arm's length, his great stature made the instrument look like a large violin, while his bow resembled the sword of a torero. His stage presence and undeniable charm were felt immediately by audiences. By his willingness to play anywhere, even in the smallest villages, he made the cello known—and loved—throughout the world. His feeling for the instrument, the inimitable, passionate sonority of his tone, his brilliant technique—all contributed to his immense popularity. After 1939, he made only a few appearances in Europe. His activities were centered in the United States where, although he continued to concertize, he devoted more and more time to teaching.

For Piatigorsky, the essential thing was music. "I am above all a musician, I do not live for success but for the music. The most difficult thing to achieve is satisfaction with myself—I have not applauded myself often." All his philosophy is summed up in these words:

> In our epoch, when everything moves very swiftly and is self-destructive, only one thing can save humanity—Art. It is Art which should be the religion of the world. To be sure, there are many religions and many gods and every one thinks that his is a little bit better than the others. By dint of comparing religions, by pitting them one against another, religious wars have inevitably resulted. Whereas, music can be compared without end, and never do the countries or friends who have different artistic conceptions go to battle in order to impose their views.
>
> I think that music as an art ought to have a more important place in our society. Of course, it seems less important than the political economy, for example, and at times even appears to be a luxury, but it is just the opposite: music is a product of human necessity.

AMATEURS

Love of the cello has frequently drawn some unexpected personalities to a study of the instrument, and a few have turned out to be amateurs

Figure 56. An unexpected cellist—the great Russian basso Feodor Chaliapin (1873–1938) in 1914.

of excellent caliber. It may be surprising to find the great Russian basso Feodor Chaliapin embracing a cello (*Figure* 56); but it is even more so to see the celebrated American actress of Hollywood's Golden Age, Bette Davis, likewise doing so. The instrument was also one of the many interests of Goethe and of Jean-Jacques Rousseau.

Quite a few of our recognized composers were cellists, too—including Christoph Willibald Gluck, Gioacchino Rossini, Jacques Offenbach, Alexander Borodin, Anton Webern, and Arnold Schoenberg.

It is remarkable that Schoenberg (1874–1951)—the man who said, "Nobody wanted to be Schoenberg, it was very essential that someone be he, so it is I!"—wrote a Cello Concerto based on a composition of Georg Matthias Monn (1717–1750). Schoenberg completely adapted this baroque work to his own style (although not in serial writing). Dedicated to Casals, who never played it, the work was introduced by Emanuel Feuermann in 1936, in the United

Figure 57. A music party made up of Frederick, Prince of Wales (1707–1751), and his sisters. Painting by Philippe Mercier, 1733. *Courtesy National Portrait Gallery, London.*

States. Although Schoenberg had been a cellist, some of the passages he wrote are nonetheless so uncellistic and awkward that their difficulty is not justified by the musical result. For this reason, the concerto is still seldom performed despite the vogue Schoenberg's music now enjoys—more than thirty years after his death.

Among illustrious orchestra conductors, Arturo Toscanini and Sir John Barbirolli were both professional cellists before taking up the baton. Various royal families have also produced cellists. The Emperor Joseph II of Austria is said to have played rather well, as is Peter II, son of Peter the Great, who was taught by Johann Riedel (1688–1775), the German fencing-master at the imperial court in St. Petersburg. Today, the cello playing of Charles, Prince of Wales is part of a family tradition established by Prince Frederick (*Figure 57*) and continued by King George III and King George IV, who was a student of Crosdill.

Figure 58. This exquisitely and profusely carved cello made by Domenico Galli bears the date 8 September 1691. Galli presented it, along with his sonatas, to Francesco II, Duke of Modena. *Courtesy Galleria Estense, Modena.*

ITALY

Amateurs have occupied an important place in the history of the cello. A great many compositions for the instrument, some of them quite beautiful (as well as some quite beautifully made instruments), would never have come into existence without their interest. The earliest among the most important of these silent partners was Francesco II, Duke of Este and Prince of Modena (1660–1694), a well informed patron who gathered many artists around him. His reign was brilliant and peaceful, but unfortunately short. The maestro di capella G. B. Vitali gave him lessons and wrote many pieces for him. He commissioned an instrument from Stradivari for his use; and on April 5, 1686, Stradivari himself delivered the cello and received from the prince not only high praise but also a bonus of thirty gold pistoles on top of the agreed price. In 1691, the prince was given a second cello, this one the work of Domenico Galli, but it is of value only as a unique collector's item (*Figure* 58). It is so excessively decorated with allegories on the religion and politics of the age—so richly carved in a way that violates all the principles of acoustics—that it is useless as a musical instrument.

Along with the cello, Galli sent the prince a collection of sonatas (for his "amusement") dedicated to him and entitled "Trattenimento musicale sopra il violoncello." It is interesting to note that these works were *sonatas* for unaccompanied cello (tuned as a *violoncello da chiesa*), the first of their genre. They were not followed by others until the early twentieth century. Another work appeared in 1687, however, four years before Galli's, which as far as we know is the first published work for solo cello. It consists of a group of études called Twelve Ricercate opus 1 by Giovanni Battista degli Antoni, probably written for a six-stringed cello of the type made by the Amati brothers—Antonio (1550–1638) and Girolamo (1551–1635), sons of Andrea (*Figure* 59). The date is important because the first known significant work for solo viola da gamba, Suite opus 9 by Johann Schenck, did not appear until 1700 and Bach did not write his Suites for unaccompanied cello until 1720.

Another composer of this period who wrote ricercare for solo cello was Domenico Gabrielli (1655–1690). He was such a special favorite

Figure 59. A small, six-stringed cello with certain features of a viol made by Antonio and Girolamo Amati in 1611. It is probable that it originally had no frets. The Twelve Ricercate of Giovanni Battista degli Antoni were probably composed for an instrument such as this. *Courtesy Hill Collection, Ashmolean Museum, Oxford.*

of Francesco II that when Gabrielli lay mortally ill in Bologna, the prince desperately sent his personal physician to "do the impossible" and save him.

In Naples, the duke of Maddaloni was an amateur cellist—probably a student of Franciscello—and a great patron of the arts. Among those in his service was Giovanni Battista Pergolesi, (1710–1736) the famed composer of the *Stabat Mater* and *La Serva Padrona*, who dedicated a sinfonia for cello and harpsichord to him. The Duke was also patron to Leonardo de Leo (1694–1744), composer, cellist, and organist who wrote six concertos in his honor in 1737 and 1738, one of which is entitled "Sinfonia Concertata." These works are among the best of the period.

GERMANY

At the same time in Germany, Count Rudolf von Schoenborn, of a family of art patrons comparable to the Medicis, held court in his sumptuous castle at Wiesentheid, where music was predominant. Fortunately, a large part of his library has been preserved, and an important number of unpublished works for cello were recently discovered there: seven concertos by Vivaldi, as well as twelve sonatas and twenty concertos by Giovanni Platti. It is almost impossible still to uncover unknown music, and the count's passion for the cello has rewarded us to this day.

In 1724 at a Viennese court ball, the orchestra was conducted by Emperor Charles VI himself, and the cello section included Count von Pergen, Count Herbenstein, and Count von Hardeck. This preponderance of titles demonstrates that the prejudice that surrounded the cello in the beginning—that it was an instrument only for "those who must work for a living"—had disappeared.

The amateur who inspired some of the most beautiful pages in cello literature was indisputably Frederick-William II of Prussia (1744–1797), successor to his uncle Frederick II, from whom he inherited his taste for music. At the time he took the Duport brothers into his service, he was studying cello with an Italian named Carlo Graziani, who was subsequently driven from the court by the arrival of the two French artists. Although this monarch managed the affairs of his country very badly—allowing its finances to lapse into a pitiful state, establishing censorship, and joining in the last two partitions of Poland—he was nevertheless the dedicatée of many admirable compositions. Among these there were fifty-six assorted works (symphonies, trios, quartets, and quintets) by Boccherini; six superb Quartets opus 50 by Haydn; and three Quartets K. 575, 589, and 590 by Mozart. These last show considerable audacity, particularly in the cello writing, which is frequently scored higher than that of the viola. The six Sonatas opus 4 that Jean-Pierre Duport dedicated to him are excellent examples of the compositional style prevalent at that time—its main objective being to make the soloist sparkle with virtuosity. The two Sonatas opus 5 for cello and piano that Beethoven wrote for him placed the cello on an equal plane with the piano for the first time; they also contain a lyricism not found in his violin or piano sonatas. Carl Stamitz (1746–1801), son of the Mannheim School's celebrated Johann Stamitz, also dedicated three cello concertos to him, the first containing a cadenza written by Duport.

RUSSIA

The cello was introduced to Russia during the late seventeenth century by Prince Golovin (c. 1670–1738), a favorite of Peter the Great, who traveled in his entourage and made the most of the opportunity this offered to study cello in Holland and Venice. Of the latter city he recalled that he did nothing there but "drink wine, smoke tobacco, and play the cello." Golovin, the first amateur cellist we know of in Russia, established a vogue for the instrument among the aristocracy that lasted for a long time. He was quickly followed by a large number of amateurs, including Baron Alexander Stroganov (1698–1754)—a name better known to gourmets—who was said to play admirably well, and Prince Nicolai Scheremetiev (1751–1809), who studied with Ivart, first cellist of the Paris Opera. These musicians met regularly at the Music Club of St. Petersburg, which was founded in 1772. Scheremetiev's beautiful Montagnana cello is on display today at his family's palace (now a museum) in Ostankino, near Moscow.

Beethoven was popular in Russia and had good friends there, but in Prince Nicolai Galitsin (1794–1866) he found his great Russian champion. On 29 January 1823, Beethoven wrote the prince a letter (in French) in which he said, "As I see that you devote yourself to the study of the cello, I am taking the trouble to indulge you in this interest," promising to compose some quartets for him. This first important Russian cellist, being a member of an illustrious family, Galitsin studied in Vienna from 1804 to 1806 while Count Rasumovsky was the Russian ambassador. At the embassy, he met other important musicians of the day as well as Beethoven, who said of the prince, "He lives for art and only for it." Galitsin was tremendously impressed with the music of Haydn, Mozart, and Beethoven; he was instrumental in introducing much of it to Russian audiences. In 1822, the prince commissioned Beethoven to write the Quartets opus 127, 130, and 132 which are conceded to be among the most beautiful in all the literature. It is insignificant that the composer could not deliver them for three or four years because he was ill and preoccupied with the Ninth Symphony.

Galitsin managed to play constantly—as a soloist, as an orchestra member, and in chamber music groups. Glinka, who particularly admired him, insisted that he take part in the premiere of his opera *A Life for the Tsar*, which was held at the residence of Prince Yusupov. Galitsin also formed an excellent quartet, which regularly toured Russia; and the Philharmonic Society of St. Petersburg entrusted him with the position of director. Under the auspices of this society, he arranged the first performance in St. Petersburg of Beethoven's *Missa Solemnis* in 1824 and was among its first twelve subscribers. A partial performance of this work had been given during the same season in Vienna, but not the complete work. The program also included the overture *The Consecration of the House* opus 124, dedicated to Galitsin.

In 1828, Galitsin founded the Society of Musical Amateurs, whose main objective was to promote concerts. They gave the first performances of many contemporary works, including the symphonies of Beethoven. Galitsin occupied a chair in the cello section of the orchestra, along with his friends Count Apraxine, Prince Radziwill, Bernhard Romberg, and Count Mathieu Vielgorsky. His house, a meeting place for the intellectuals of St. Petersburg, was open to all artists, musicians, painters, and poets. While visiting Russia in 1839, the marquis de Custine attended one of the gatherings where he was vociferous in his praise both of the hospitality and of the cello playing of the master of the house.

At the frequent sessions of chamber music in which Galitsin participated, the works of Beethoven naturally took a prominent place. On 29 November 1822, he wrote to the composer, "I value enormously everything that comes from your pen and I have all that you have composed so far for the piano, as well as for other instruments. In my free moments I enjoy transcribing some of your marvelous sonatas for string quartet." When Beethoven died, Galitsin had these arrangements published as a memorial to him, stipulating that all profit be given to needy musicians.

Galitsin's eclecticism showed itself in his literary faculties. Visiting Paris in 1814, he met many artists and writers of the day and familiarized himself with French so well that he could make one of the first translations into this language of the works of Pushkin—with the blessing of the poet.

The cellist Elie Lisogoub (1787–1867) was the first Russian composer to write a sonata for cello and piano. He dedicated it to his brother-in-law Count Andrei Gudovitch, an impassioned amateur who gave it its first performance in 1825 on his Stradivarius. A great uncle to my great uncle, Gudovitch became the first director of the Moscow Musical Society, as well as one of its founders, and took an active part in the musical life of his time. He played regularly in quartet concerts; and as a soloist, he performed works as difficult as the Romberg Variations. In 1863, he gave his superb cello to my great uncle, Senator Andrei Markevitch, himself an excellent cellist, who succeeded Gudovitch as director of the Russian Musical Society (*see Figure 26*). This society played a major role in the development of music in Russia. Under its auspices, a complete network of concerts across the country was instituted; it commissioned works from composers of that time and promoted their publication. The organization was divided into two principal groups, one in St. Petersburg and the other in Moscow, which formed the bases of the conservatories founded in these cities—one under the direction of Anton Rubinstein, the other under his brother Nicholas. Smaller groups were responsible for establishing music schools in Kiev and other Russian cities. With the cooperation of such musicians as violinists Henri Wieniawski and Leopold Auer and cellists Karl Davidov and von Glehn, the society maintained permanent professional quartets in residence in Moscow, Kiev, and St. Petersburg.

The Russian appetite for music grew to be intense and insatiable. During the last century, the Czech cellist Heinrich Grunfeld (1855–1931) made many concert tours there and offered the following comments on the programming and decorum of the time:

> The people in Russia cry out and let their passions run wild, to the extent that one could think they had gone crazy. It is incredible what they are able to engulf in the way of music. I have seen a presentation of a Glinka opera at the Grand Theatre in St. Petersburg where,

> during the first intermission Sarasate played the entire Violin Concerto of Beethoven, during the second—the entire Mendelssohn Concerto, and during the third—a group of pieces from his own repertoire, followed by encores. It is not astonishing then that these soirées lasted long into the night. Consequently, if one wishes to please this public, it is necessary that programs last many hours and cover a time period which goes beyond the capacity of any European to absorb. At the end of the concert, at 1 or 2 A.M., everyone goes to a reception, and if someone wishes to say good-bye to the mistress of the house around seven or eight in the morning, she is very surprised that one is leaving so soon. During these soirées one eats and drinks enormously, and this type of obligatory invitation after a concert makes the entire evening extremely exhausting. In addition, it is not only *comme il faut* to invite the artists, but it is a practice to always give them expensive presents.

Count Mathieu Vielgorsky (1794–1866) was an exact contemporary of Galitsin, and just as important a cellist as he (*Figure* 60). Born in St. Petersburg into a home where music was played constantly, his first participation consisted of turning pages for a quartet made up of his father and his three older brothers, all excellent musicians. After living with his family in various places—Riga, Vienna, and Paris (where Bernhard Romberg made a deep impression on him)—he returned to Russia where he began to study cello in earnest with Adolph Meingardt. Sometime during this period, he met Galitsin and a lifelong friendship began. Throughout the Napoleonic wars, he was a member of the elite cavalry regiment of the Imperial Guard, a service that lasted until 1826. After the downfall of Napoleon, he was enrolled in the Allied Army of Occupation and found himself once again in Paris. Despite his military service, he had not abandoned his beloved cello; so he was able to profit greatly from the opportunity to associate with celebrated Parisian musicians.

Highly prized as a quartet player, Vielgorsky was much in demand for chamber music sessions. His brother Michael, a talented composer whom Schumann called an "amateur of genius," organized musical evenings at his estate in Louisino in which Mathieu participated with almost a desperate eagerness. During 1822 alone, thirty-three concerts were given there. The programs were well chosen, comprising

Figure 60. Count Mathieu Yurevitch Vielgorsky (1794–1866), in a portrait from 1828 by K. Brullow.

symphonic and chamber works of Beethoven, Mozart, Boccherini, Rossini, and others, as well as compositions by the Vielgorsky brothers themselves. Mathieu later settled in Moscow, where he organized a group of well-attended concerts in which he often collaborated with the English pianist and composer John Field, the inventor of the nocturne, who preceded Chopin. Bernhard Romberg, for whom he had a profound admiration, frequently played duets of his own composition with him. Mathieu knew practically all of Romberg's work and often performed his concertos and his Fantasy on Russian Airs. Deciding that Vielgorsky interpreted his compositions better than any other important cellist, the composer dedicated his Seventh Concerto to him. Out of this mutual regard for their art, the two men became friends; and Romberg lived in the Prince's palace during the two years he spent in Russia.

On his return from Paris, Vielgorsky and a group of friends founded the St. Petersburg branch of the Russian Musical Society, which he directed for many years. His home became the scene of frequent musical soirées enlisting the greatest talent of the day. Romberg, Servais, Wieniawski, and Field took part in these evenings, as at various times did Glinka, Liszt, Berlioz, Verdi, Wagner, Vieuxtemps, and Anton Rubinstein. Berlioz developed a great respect for Vielgorsky's activities, saying, "The house of this ardent and intelligent champion of music is a real musical sanctuary." For selected audiences, in which Pushkin was often to be found, Vielgorsky and the composer played the sonatas written for him by Joseph Genichta (1795–1853). He received Robert Schumann and his wife with extreme cordiality, eliciting from Clara the statement, "Vielgorsky is extraordinary for artists. He lives only for art and does not look for any profit whatsoever." The Piano Quartet opus 7 that Schumann wrote for him contains an interesting and rewarding cello part. Its premiere performance occurred at the Leipzig Gewandhaus in 1844, with Clara Schumann, Ferdinand David, Niels Gade, and Vielgorsky.

Francois Servais and Henri Wieniawski also dedicated works to Vielgorsky, as did Mendelssohn, who wrote his Sonata opus 58 for him, and joined him in its first performance while it was still in manuscript. Later, Vielgorsky often played it with other pianists—including Clara Schumann and Anton Rubinstein.

At a memorable concert in St. Petersburg in 1842, Franz Liszt, Alexis Lvov, and Vielgorsky played trios by both Beethoven and Schubert. Lvov, who was director of the Imperial Chapel, also joined V. Maurer, G. Wild, and Vielgorsky in forming a quartet that performed many of the great classics with much success.

This exceptional personality, whose talent was widely recognized, toured Europe playing in all the principal cities of Italy. In 1828, he appeared in Paris; and in Berlin the music critic of the *Neue Berliner Musikzeitung* wrote of his astonishment at seeing someone play "from memory"—Vielgorsky being one of the first to introduce this custom. Mendelssohn called him a "true artist" and Giacomo Meyerbeer, whom he met while vacationing at Spa, professed to be "completely dumbfounded" on hearing a concert of Glinka's works which Vielgorsky had arranged.

Being an amateur only in that he had no need to earn a living as a musician, he was also an excellent colleague—recommending and promoting such virtuosi as Alfredo Piatti and Alexander Batta, whom he presented to the Russian public. Many renowned cellists received expensive instruments from him as gifts. A year before his death, he gave his own beautiful Stradivarius to the celebrated cellist Karl Davidov. He left his impressive collection of music scores to the St. Petersburg Conservatory. This "very humble servant" of music died on 21 February 1866 at Nice, his favorite vacation spot.

To list all the other cellists who were part of this purely Russian phenomenon—the "aristocratic musicians" of the last century—would be tedious. Pampered by life and endowed with all its material blessings, they nonetheless took advantage of their gifts in a constructive way. They practiced their art with utmost seriousness, founded all kinds of musical societies, formed orchestras, organized concerts, invited foreign artists to tour Russia, and contributed greatly to the promotion of new compositions and to music in general. Their intense interest undoubtedly was responsible for developing many excellent musicians.

Figure 61. The numbers above the lower (bass) staff are typical of the figured bass notation of the later eighteenth century. This example is the opening bars of Sonata III for cello and continuo from opus 2 (1770) by Louis Janson (1749–1815).

Great Moments for the Cello

EVOLUTION AND TECHNICAL DEVELOPMENT

THE CELLIST'S MISSION is to keep alive treasures of beautiful music that would otherwise sleep forever. For this the cello is a marvelous means of expression, ideal for transmitting a message; but the content of this message must have real significance. Therefore, we must acquaint ourselves with the great moments for cello in music—complete works and isolated passages—whose deep meaning will be revealed to us by the performer through his talent and his personality. What follows is a panorama of these compositions.

At first, the cello was used solely as an accompanying instrument. Its principal function was to play the "continuo" or "thorough-bass" line (continued bass line), a part that helps to support the melodic line. Eventually, numbers were placed above this bass line, and it came to be known as *figured bass*—the method used during the baroque period (1600–1750). Figured bass is a type of musical shorthand whose purpose is to indicate to the accompanying instrumentalists what specific intervals or chords are to be added to the simply stated bass line in order to build the desired harmony: *4* for a fourth, *6* for a sixth, *7* for a seventh, and so on. For chromatic alterations, a sharp or a flat is placed in front of the number concerned (*Figure 61*).

This is only a very brief description to illustrate how elaborate the art of accompanying had become as it extended the improvisational techniques of the sixteenth century—in which no numbers were added and the performer was allowed total freedom.

As a rule, figured bass was played on the harpsichord, the viola da gamba or the cello playing the lower part in unison with the left hand of the harpsichordist. Because the harpsichord was incapable of sustaining a tone, a bowed instrument was needed to prolong the sound. In many instances, musicians preferred to have only a cello accompany them. In addition, harpsichords were not always available. Such was the case with Arcangelo Corelli (1653–1713), the great Italian violinist and composer of well-known sonatas and concerti grossi, who preferred to play his compositions with a cellist—possibly Gaetano Boni. Guiseppe Tartini (1692–1770), known for his famous "Devil's Trill," was always accompanied by the cellist Antonio Vandini (1690–c. 1771), with whom he was friends for fifty years (Vandini followed Tartini to Prague when he went there in 1723 at the invitation of the chancellor). It was the same with Francisco Veracini (1690–1750), an outstanding violin virtuoso who gave numerous concerts with the renowned Neapolitan cellist Salvatore Lanzetti (c. 1710–1780) as his accompanist. As a soloist himself, Lanzetti was warmly received in Paris in 1736 at the Concert Spirituel. He later went on to London, where he lived for many years and did much to bring the cello into favor in England.

These excellent cellists, who had a sound knowledge of harmony, often indulged themselves in excessive improvisations. They added a great profusion of ornaments—trills, mordents, and other figures—melodic embellishments used to make long notes more interesting and to emphasize important harmonic transitions. Although composers sometimes indicated what ornaments were to be used, often they left the choice to the performer. In the *Clavier-Büchlein*, for example, J. S. Bach gave this explicit explanation of the realization of his notation to his son W. F. Bach. He wrote this in 1720, at exactly the time he composed the Suites for Unaccompanied Cello (*Figure* 62).

The use of these figures was encouraged by opinions such as that of Jean Rousseau in his *Traité de la viole* (Paris, 1687): "Embellishments are the melodic salt which seasons the music, which gives it flavor,

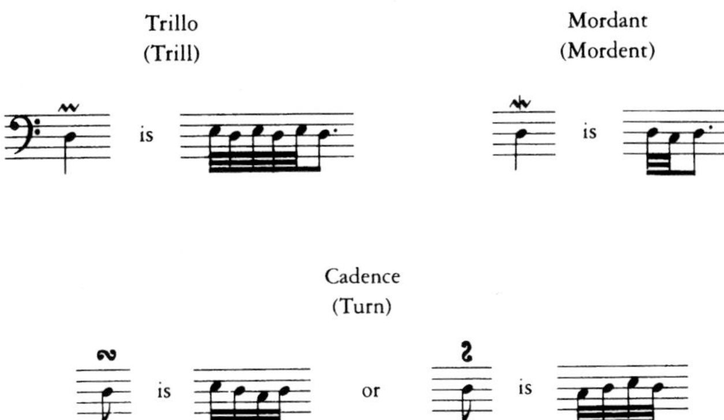

Figure 62. The indications for ornaments that Johann Sebastian Bach gave to his son Wilhelm Friedemann in *Das Klavier Büchlein*, written in 1720 when the cello suites were being composed.

and without which it would be dull and insipid." Musicians of the baroque era often went to such exaggerated lengths, however, that the result was a complete distortion of the work. Thus authors were obliged to remind performers of the mandate: "Imagination invents the ornaments but good taste restricts them."[1]

In the evolution of the cello's role in music, four functional stages can be observed—successive periods that did not supplant each other but were added one after the other, until a role evolved that embraced all four stages in a parallel way. This is the role in which we see the cello functioning today.

In the first stage, the cello took the part of the continuo and made only rare attempts to depart from the given line.

In the second, it began to take a little liberty, combining its own harmony with the basso, playing—sometimes on the octave, sometimes alone or with another instrument—a melodic line that contained some elements of counterpoint.

In the third, it became independent and no longer played conjointly with its partners. It was accompanied in its own right by a harpsichord or other continuo.

1. Baillot, Levasseur, Catel, et Baudiot, *Méthode de violoncelle* (Paris, 1804).

In the fourth, or final stage, it had total freedom and might play alone, as the solo instrument in a concerto, as a partner of equal importance in a duo (sonata), or as part of an ensemble with complete technical liberty. This is the role in which we see the cello functioning today.

This evolution was not without setbacks, but it was favored by the appearance of talented performers who caused it to make successive leaps forward.

The first attempts to give a little independence to the cello appeared with the Italian composers of the second part of the seventeenth century. Even though their experiments were at first optional—as with the Bolognese Guido Arresti (c. 1630–c. 1695), or with Giovanni Battista Bassani (1657–1716) in his sonatas for two violins, cello ad libitum, and organ—they are proof of an undeniable trend which, although subject to some temporary eclipses, has now become totally accepted and frequently favored by contemporary composers.

At the time of the creation of an academy for men of letters and musicians by Lorenzo di Medici in Florence, various intellectual circles were flourishing across Europe. In France, Jean Antoine de Baïf had founded the *Academie de Musique et de Poésie* in Paris in 1567, while in Bologna, a city whose musical activities had been flourishing for a long time, the most important organization of the epoch was founded in 1666—the *Accademia Filarmonica*, an elite society with severe requirements for admission, which controlled the artistic affairs of the region for two centuries. Among its members were some eminent composers. Corelli studied at Bologna and was admitted to the academy in 1670 before he settled in Rome. Exactly one hundred years later, Mozart became a member. Among other prominent musicians admitted to the Accademia, one finds the names of Padre Martini, Rossini, and Busoni.

Spirited concerts, meetings, and discussions were held at the Accademia; but it was not the only musical center in the area—there was also tremendous activity at the Basilica San Petronio. This huge church—unfinished because the Bolognese, who had hoped to make it grander than St. Peters in Rome, ran out of funds—had two organs facing each other in the nave. Services held here were conducted with great pomp and ceremony; and the *maestro di cappella*, with a first-class orchestra at his disposal, was expected to produce music suitable for each occasion. He did, however, have freedom of choice in the matter of the works played. In contrast, the musicians at the neighboring city of Modena were dependent on the whim of their prince. Nevertheless, there was much interchange between the two cities, and certain festivals were organized jointly.

Among the Bolognese musicians, there were some remarkable cellists—such as Petronio Franceschini (1650–1681), the first to be engaged with a regular salary at San Petronio, and his celebrated pupil Domenico Gabrielli (1655–1690), whose contemporaries nicknamed him (in the local dialect) "*il Mingain dal Viulunzeel*—Dominic the cellist." He was the first to reveal, in a brilliant way, the enormous possibilities of the cello. He was also the first composer to use the cello as an obligato instrument in the accompaniment of opera arias. If Corelli was called "father of the modern violin," Gabrielli was the "Corelli of the cello." His lyric sense and his feeling for expression were particularly evident in his Ricercari for unaccompanied cello (1689). These works—the first of this genre—together with those of G. B. degli Antoni—show a thorough knowledge of the cello's potential. Another first for Gabrielli was his composition in 1689 of two sonatas for cello and continuo, one in G major and one in A. Gabrielli's maturity as a musician is apparent in both. He made use of all the cellistic technique known at that time, and his writing closely resembles the violin music of Corelli. Considering the atmosphere of intense musical activity in Bologna, it is not astonishing that it became the birthplace of these innovative works for cello.

Gabrielli had a short but eventful life: he was made a member of the Accademia Filarmonica when barely seventeen and became its president at twenty-four. At the age of twenty-one (following the death of Franceschini) he became solo cellist at San Petronio. While there, he composed a large number of diverse works—oratorios, cantatas, a dozen operas, some sonatas for trumpet, and other instrumental works. In addition, he was head of the San Petronio orchestra. In the musical centers of Europe, he was greatly admired not only for his talent as a cellist but for his skill as a composer. Francesco d'Este held him in high regard and regularly invited him to play at Modena.

Other cellists from Bologna were Giovanni Battista Vitali (1644–1692), Giacomo Perti (1661–1756), Giuseppe Jacchini (c. 1660–1727) who wrote some interesting sonatas for cello and continuo, and Giovanni Bononcini (1670–1747), famous for his quarrels with Handel in England. Through his travels across Europe, Bononcini became known as a successful cellist; and in 1733, he made a notable debut in Paris. He also gained renown as a composer of oratorios, operas, and duos for his own instrument.

The year 1700 marked the beginning of a rich period in the literature of the cello. It has been estimated that more than fifteen hundred sonatas were written before 1796, the date of Beethoven's first sonatas. I will be content to describe the most significant of these in the section dealing with chamber music. Lovers of the cello—including (I think) the professionals—will certainly be amazed to realize the significance of the material in certain areas of our repertoire that is still unexplored.

THE IMPORTANT CONCERTOS

Since the end of World War II, there has been a great revival of interest in the music of Antonio Vivaldi (1678–1741), an awareness due especially to the remarkable studies of the French musicologist Marc Pincherle. Although he has literally put Vivaldi back in fashion, this craze does not seem to have affected cellists. They are satisfied to continue playing just one or two concertos or—even more frequently—an arrangement for cello and orchestra of the fifth Sonata for cello and continuo. This scorn for the man who wrote the first bona fide concertos for our instrument is absolutely inexplicable, especially considering that he wrote twenty-eight of them! Even though they are not all of equal quality, they still contain much beautiful music. Composed for his pupils—the young women at the Conservatorio dell'Ospedale della Pieta in Venice—and probably played by Antonio Vandini, the cello professor there—some of them present genuine problems of technical interest. They may have been conceived for a cello tuned in this way:

as in the works of D. Gabrielli and his contemporaries.

Vivaldi was ordained as a priest in 1703, but illness (apparently tuberculosis) prevented him from practicing his ministry; so he was able to concentrate on music. Incredibly prolific, he composed an enormous quantity of diverse works, a large proportion of them unknown until fifty years ago when the Library of Turin received a gift of many of his unpublished manuscripts. Most of the cello concertos were part of this group although a few more works have recently been discovered at Wiesentheid. These works are part of an incredible body of 454 concertos for different instruments, including the viola d'amour, the mandolin, and the piccolo. Although the modern Italian composer Luigi Dallipiccola has called Vivaldi "the composer of the same concerto six hundred times," on hearing his works one quickly perceives that this ready witticism is ill-founded. For example, his originality is revealed in the Concerto in E minor, which opens with the solo cello accompanied by a bassoon—a unique choice. In addition, this concerto has a novel characteristic in its tempo markings. In the first movement, solos are marked *adagio* and tuttis *allegro*, while in the second movement it is just the reverse—*allegro* for the cello and *adagio* for the orchestral interludes. In the third movement, there is the same *allegro* marking for all. This gives evidence of the inquiring mind Vivaldi brought to his music, which Bach admired so greatly. Even if his type of writing did not reach the heights attained by some other late eighteenth-century composers, he was already exploiting the cello's potential for virtuosity in a significant way. In addition, in his slow movements, Vivaldi gave his soloists a pure line—tender or dramatic—that could be sung with emotion. He was thus the first to introduce the expressive style of playing.

Next we find the interesting concertos of Leonardo Leo, who is discussed elsewhere in this book. To these must be added a number of concertos—most of which are still in manuscript, scattered among different libraries—of composers such as Nicola Porpora, Antonio Vandini, Domenico Lanzetti, Giovanni Platti (whose twenty concertos are still unpublished), and many others. Among those works available in good modern editions, it is necessary to single out the concertos of Giovanni Battista Cirri (1724–1808) and Luigi Borghi (c. 1745–c. 1800). The latter wrote a charming Concerto in D major, which Jean-Louis Duport played with success at the Concert Spirituel in 1788.

Giuseppe Tartini (1692–1770), one of the great violinists of the eighteenth century, composer, acoustician, theorist, and author of two interesting essays, "Treatise on Ornaments in Music" and "The Art of the Bow," wrote two concertos for cello which deserve to be heard more often. Probably composed for his friend Vandini, one is in D major and the other is in A.[2] Of the two, the D major has the more elaborate writing, but both have another peculiarity in common—the cadenzas are written out by the composer. This was most unusual in an age when soloists were allowed—and expected—to improvise their own. The cadenzas in the D major Concerto are called "capriccios," the one in the second movement lasting for eighteen measures while the one in the final movement extends through the exceptional length of fifty measures.

The second son of J. S. Bach, Carl Philipp Emanuel (1714–1788), *Kapellmeister* at the court of Frederick II of Prussia, composed three concertos—those in A minor, B♭ major, and A major. The last, if only for its admirable *Lento mesto*, which reaches rare heights of lyricism, is worthy of performance.

The marvelous music of Boccherini is alas still known principally through two works—his celebrated Minuet, which has been arranged in every possible fashion, and the Cello Concerto in B♭ G.482, which is still generally heard in a version that has little resemblance to the original score. This edition is an irreverent arrangement—actually a total redrafting of the composition by the German cellist of the last century, Friedrich Grützmacher, who completely distorted it. He replaced the entire second movement with an Adagio—albeit a beautiful one—from another of Boccherini's concertos, to which he made some additions of his own. The first and last movements were handled with extreme liberty. They contain many changes, as well as excerpts from other Boccherini works and tuttis from Grützmacher's own pen. The whole is reorchestrated in a "St. Sulpice" style, to the point where

2. The original manuscript of the first concerto is in Vienna in the archives of the Gesellschaft der Musikfreunde; the autograph of the second is in the Archivio Musicale della Veneranda Arca del Santo in Padova.

it becomes a work more "in the manner of" than "by" Boccherini. He really did not deserve that!

If I treat Grützmacher somewhat as a scapegoat, it is primarily to emphasize the paramount importance of good editions and to stress the importance of eliminating the bad ones. What was accepted fifty years ago is no longer admissible today. Over the past twenty years, musicology has made enormous progress. It is now essential that the gap between musicologists and performers be completely abolished so that most practicing musicians are brought up to date with the latest research and discoveries of the specialists. Too many musical masterworks are still in danger. Meanwhile, *Urtext* editions (reproductions of original scores) are being published in increasing numbers, and some excellent dissertations throw new light on the interpretation of the music of different periods. As a result, we can entertain the hope that a certain "musical ecology" may soon be understood.

Boccherini holds a very important place in the history of the cello, being one of its major composers as well as one of its great virtuosos. He made tremendous advances in the technique of the instrument and thereby put it on an equal footing with the violin and other solo instruments. Naturally, all his compositions are marvelously suitable for the instrument; and although they are often extremely difficult (frequently lying entirely in the high register), they always show the cello to good advantage. In addition, the artist can display his virtuosity in the rapid movements and sing in the slow passages. One typical example of Boccherini's style is the Concerto in D major G.483, in which the second movement, *Andante lentarello*, contains a lovely original cadenza. Another is the Concerto in E♭ major G.474, which ends with a charming rondo—written in a key rarely used in those days because it was considered uncomfortable for the performer. In choosing this key, however, the composer gives a shining example of his extraordinary knowledge of the instrument. The E♭ major tonality is cleverly used and sounds admirably well in this work. In his ravishing Concerto in G major G.480, there is the superb Adagio ravaged by Grützmacher. As I have explained previously, Boccherini is still practically unknown—his eleven interesting concertos for cello have yet to be published in their entirety. This is deplorable, but let us hope it will not be long before they are all available.

Under the impetus of Berteau and the Duport brothers, the French School was active in the second half of the eighteenth century. A great deal was written for the instrument, and cellists in particular revealed much talent for composition. Among those who wrote concertos—François Cupis, Janson, the Duport brothers, and others—the most interesting was probably Jean Baptiste Bréval (1753–1823), one of the first to teach at the Paris Conservatoire. His pleasant music, reminiscent of the spirit of Jean-Jacques Rousseau, is fresh and full of vivacity, and his Concertos (in G major, D major, and particularly the seventh in A major) are admirably written for the cello.

Among so many others, from four countries, in France were the three concertos of Ignaz Pleyel, founder of the famous firm of piano builders and music publishers; in England, those of John Garth; in Germany those of Carl Stamitz (mentioned previously) and Peter Ritter; and in Austria, those of Georg Matthias Monn and Georg Christopher Wagenseil.

It was with Franz Joseph Haydn (1732–1809), however, that the first major concertos in our repertoire appeared. Of the four concertos listed in the catalogue of his complete works, only two are available today, one in C major Hob. VIIb no. 1 and the other in D major op. 101, Hob. VIIb no. 2. Each of these works has been the victim of different vicissitudes. The first was actually lost for many years, being rediscovered in 1961 at the Library of the National Museum of Prague in a collection of manuscripts from Radenin Castle. Probably written around 1765, the Concerto in C major must have been played by Joseph Weigl, cellist in the Esterhazy orchestra from 1761 to 1769 and a good friend of Haydn, who was godfather to his son. It is one of the first concertos for cello by this great composer, and it is typical of the compositions of his youth; it is both brilliant and well written for the instrument, and the cadenzas in the solo part of the first and second movements (perhaps composed by Weigl) are typical of the epoch.

The Concerto in D major is the more important work. It shows more maturity, and its second movement soars to lofty summits on a melodic line of great inspiration. For many years, this work was known only through the questionable edition of the Belgian musicologist François Auguste Gevaert, director of the Brussels Conservatory at the end of the last century. Although he was not so extreme as Grützmacher, Gevaert nevertheless took many liberties with this music—amputating certain passages, adding others of his own invention, altering some of the rhythmic patterns, and entirely revising the original orchestration—to which he added flutes, clarinets, and bassoons—instruments not intended by Haydn. In 1837, the German musicologist Gustav Schilling stated that in the absence of an original manuscript it was his opinion that the cello part of the concerto was too well written to be the work of a composer who was not himself a cellist. Under the circumstances, Anton Kraft was thought to be the composer; and this legend persisted for more than a century, firmly fixed in the public mind. The discovery of a manuscript in Haydn's own hand in 1954 finally set the record straight. On the other hand, it is absolutely certain that Kraft gave the work its premiere, very likely in Vienna in 1783—the year of its composition. In 1804, the first edition, under the opus number 101, was published simultaneously by the firms of André at Offenbach and Vernay at Charenton. At the time this concerto was written, Kraft was a member of the Esterhazy orchestra and Haydn was its director. Haydn also composed a vast number of works (about 175) for the *baryton*, an instrument of the viol family popular in the eighteenth century, which was fitted with sympathetic strings like the viola d'amore and was a particular favorite of Prince Esterhazy. These works, mostly divertimentos for two barytons and cello, were played by the Prince himself, Haydn, and Kraft. The popularity of the baryton was ephemeral (almost all these compositions have since fallen into oblivion); but the success of the Concerto in D has never faltered, and to this day, it retains merited favor with cellists and music lovers alike.

In addition to Boccherini and Haydn, the classical period (1750–1830) produced works of lesser composers like the Krafts (father and son) and Bernhard Romberg. Fortune never smiled on Mozart's attempts to write for the cello. On two occasions, he began work on cello concertos but inexplicably left them unfinished. In 1779, he began a Sinfonia Concertante in A major for violin, viola, and cello, but only a large part of the first movement remains—the rest was never completed.

The Concerto in C major opus 4 by Anton Kraft is strongly reminiscent of the one by Haydn in the same key. It is very long and very elaborate, the writing for the solo part is difficult but well-suited to the instrument, and the whole endeavor is manifestly the work of a virtuoso. The second movement, entitled "Romanza," displays a fairly well developed lyric sense, while the "Rondo alla Cosacca," which ends the work with obvious humor and brilliance, is deftly wrought. An original cadenza, based on a childish tune, leads into the final coda.

As we have noted earlier, Bernhard Romberg preferred playing his own works to playing those of other composers. He wrote ten concertos, three concertinos, one concertino for two cellos, and some variations for cello and orchestra. These works are not without quality, and they deserve to be rescued from the ghetto in which they were confined under the excuse that they are good only as pedagogical material. Conceived with a great strictness of form, entirely classic in style, and remarkably written for the instrument, these concertos are good examples of the music of the period. Romberg naturally suffers in comparison with his greater contemporaries—notably Beethoven—even though Romberg's slow movements, in which the melody is usually beautiful, often reach a higher elevation of spirit than one finds in Beethoven's Romances for violin. Certain rapid sections of Romberg's works are written in forms such as *fandango* or *alla Polacca*. His Sixth Concerto carries the subtitle "Military," and his opus 78 is known as the "Swiss" Concerto.

Because of Romberg's shortcomings, Ludwig van Beethoven (1770–1827) never wrote a concerto for the cello; but he did give a beautiful part to the instrument in the Triple Concerto for piano, violin, and cello with orchestra opus 56, investing it with the duty of introducing the first theme of each movement. Written in the same year as the "Eroica," it is an important work—one of few composed for this combination of instruments. The cello part was intended for his friend Anton Kraft who, with Archduke Rudolph at the piano and the violinist Carl August Seidler, gave the first private performance in the winter of 1805–1806. The official premiere took place in Leipzig on 25 March 1836 (nine years after the composer's death), with the soloists Felix Mendelssohn, Ferdinand David, and Johann Grabau—a pupil of F. A. Kummer and solo cellist of the Gewandhaus Orchestra.

In the matter of concertos for the cello, the romantic period is more an era of quality than one of quantity. We have only a half-dozen great concertos from this epoch—a circumstance that considerably limits cellists' participation in symphonic programs since romantic music holds so important a place there. Perhaps this is the reason for the myth that the cello has a small repertoire. As for the nineteenth century, while it was a good deal less rich than the eighteenth had been or the twentieth was to be, it nevertheless produced several hundred concertos of minor importance. The cellists themselves were very productive, from Romberg (about whom I have already spoken) to Julius Klengel, with dozens of other celebrated virtuosos in between. Some of their works are of a quality comparable to the violin concertos of the two violinists Henri Wieniawski (1835–1880) and Henri Vieuxtemps (1820–1881). There are two compositions for cello from the latter, Concertos opus 46 and opus 50. The Russian pianist and composer Anton Rubinstein (1829–1894) also composed two Concertos for cello opus 65 and opus 96.

The first romantic concerto of importance is without doubt that of Robert Schumann (1810–1856). Composed in 1850 in Düsseldorf, near the end of his life and during a period when his health and mental state were beginning to show signs of imminent deterioration, it has a feverish quality almost aflame with the romanticism so admirably appropriate for the cello. Definitely more successful than his Violin Concerto, and more original in conception than his Piano Concerto because of its arresting musical ideas, this Cello Concerto also had the benefit of technical advice from Schumann's friend, the cellist Robert Bockmühl (1820–1881). The first performance was given by Ludwig Ebert in 1860, four years after Schumann's death.

Figure 63. Joseph Hollmann (1852–1926) was a Belgian cellist to whom Saint-Saëns dedicated his Second Cello Concerto. As a child, the French cellist Pierre Fournier lived in the same building as Hollmann. He recalls hearing horrible scraping noises emanating from the old artist's apartment as he practiced.

Camille Saint-Saëns (1835–1921) composed two Concertos, the A minor opus 33 in 1873 and the D minor opus 119 in 1902 (*Figure* 63). The first is deservedly the more popular. Wonderfully well written, in three sections played without pause, it is a flattering, grateful work to play. It presents no great technical problems, and it has some pretty lyric passages, particularly in the second section.

The Concerto of Edouard Lalo gives clear evidence of a vast knowledge of the cello, information gained by the composer through his own serious study of the instrument. This is particularly manifest in virtuoso passages that lie marvelously "under the hand." Although this work has passed out of favor, it deserves to be heard more often.

Jules Massenet (1842–1912), another French composer of the same period (celebrated for his opera *Manon*), wrote a brilliant Fantasie for cello and orchestra in 1897.

The Rococo Variations opus 33 of Peter Ilyitch Tchaikovsky

(1840–1893)—a charming evocation of the baroque style—although difficult, are remarkably conceived for the instrument. Composed in 1876 in honor of Wilhelm Fitzenhagen (1843–1890), a professor at the Moscow Conservatory, this work suffered some vicissitudes at the hands of the dedicatée, who had expected to receive an impressive concerto in the romantic vein rather than this ravishing diversion. Taking advantage of the composer's sojourn in Switzerland, Fitzenhagen revised the variations and changed their order, omitted part of the final coda, modified all the nuances, added some accents, and increased some of the dynamic markings from piano to forte. After giving the first performance in Moscow without the knowledge of the composer, he sent the score—just as he had revised it—to an editor who published it in that version. Since that time, it has been played in this edition, but a new edition recently issued in Moscow conforms to the original score. In 1976, I was able to give its first performances in France and Scandinavia.

Incontestably the greatest success of the romantic repertoire for cello is the Concerto in B minor opus 104 by Antonin Dvořák (1841–1904). It was composed in 1895; and when Brahms saw the score, shortly before his death, he said, "If I had only known that one could write a cello concerto like this, I would have composed one a long time ago!" Written for Hanus Wihan, the concerto was eventually the cause of a quarrel between Dvořák and the cellist and suffered a fate similar to that of the Rococo Variations of Tchaikovsky. It was composed during Dvořák's stay in New York (1892–1895); and when Wihan received the manuscript in Prague, he took it upon himself to make certain changes in order to render it more "virtuoso." For example, he replaced one passage with arpeggios of his own writing and introduced a long cadenza for the cello. When Dvořák learned of these revisions, he forbade Wihan to give the premiere performance; and the concerto was first presented by the English cellist Leo Stern (1862–1909) in London in 1896 under the composer's direction. Not realizing precisely how much damage had been inflicted on the work, Dvořák wrote to his editor to stop publication unless the Wihan cadenza was omitted. The cadenza was taken out, but Wihan's other changes remained, and this is the version played today, even though an edition published some time ago in Czechoslovakia adheres to Dvořák's original conception. Nonetheless, this concerto is one of the monuments of the repertoire. It is marvelously written in that the solo instrument can be heard throughout. Even though the orchestration is full and rich, the balance between soloist and orchestra is always skillfully maintained. It is a very satisfying work to play, one that recaptures its merited success at each performance.

Before arriving at the twentieth century, two outstanding works remained to be described: the Double Concerto for violin and cello opus 102, composed by Johannes Brahms (1833–1897) in 1887, and *Don Quixote* of Richard Strauss (1864–1949) written in 1897.

The Brahms is a grandiose realization in which the cello assumes the role of a lion, entering alone—after four introductory measures in the orchestra—with an imperious and majestic cadenza. Then, in the last movement, again alone, it introduces the main theme. Throughout the entire work, the dialogue between the two instruments is worked out in a masterly fashion; and the orchestra interludes occur only during periods of rest for the soloists.

The symphonic poem of Strauss, subtitled *Fantastic Variations on a Theme of Knightly Chivalry*, is a typical piece of program music in which the cello portrays the Knight of the Mournful Countenance, the violin is Dulcinea, and the viola is Sancho Panza. The ten variations depict the various adventures of Cervantes's hero, including the attack on the windmills. Nor does this descriptive music neglect the bleating of sheep or the howl of the wind. In the midst of all this anecdotal confusion, there are some moments of beautiful music, particularly in the fifth variation during the big cadenza for cello with orchestral accompaniment and at the finale, when the cello sighs out the dying breath of Don Quixote.

Among the numerous concertos of the romantic period which have been relegated to the rank of curiosities, I would like to mention a few that deserve to be given a better fate. First come the concertos of Karl Davidov, in particular the second in A minor opus 14, which Pablo Casals played frequently at the beginning of his career and which he programmed on his Russian tour in 1912. Second is the Concerto in

D minor opus 193 of Joachim Raff (1822–1882), a composer almost forgotten today who had much glory in his own time. Born in Lachen, Switzerland, he studied with Mendelssohn and became a friend of Liszt, for whom he was secretary, orchestrator, and copyist. A prolific composer, he wrote more than 250 works, some of which deserve to be heard. He also made a piano transcription of the six Suites for unaccompanied cello of Bach. Finally, the violinist and composer Bernhard Molique (1802–1869), a pupil of Spohr, wrote a Cello Concerto in D opus 45, which was a war horse to the cellists of the last century. It has been compared to the Violin Concerto of Mendelssohn, with which—for a time—it enjoyed almost equal popularity.

The number of concertos for cello composed between 1900 and today can be estimated in the neighborhood of five hundred. I myself have eighty-six good ones in my library. Much as I would like to discuss even the most representative, they are so numerous (fifty concertos from thirty-eight different composers) that it would be tedious to describe them all in detail. I must be content with listing them in chronological order in the table on pages 140 and 141.

CHAMBER MUSIC

At the beginning of the eighteenth century, even though a certain degree of independence had been granted to the use of the cello, its role in chamber music was still limited to an association with the continuo. Meanwhile, as the performers began to develop greater facility of execution and artists like Franciscello became widely known, the composers of the day—as well as the cellists themselves—would inevitably begin to write for the instrument. Those living in Italy and France were particularly active.

In 1717, Gaetano Boni, whose dates are unknown but who was active between 1717 and 1741 and was a member of the Accademia Filarmonica at Bologna, dedicated his Twelve Sonatas opus 1, to Cardinal Ottoboni, Corelli's benefactor. Although showing the influence of both D. Gabrielli and Corelli, these rather interesting works display a feeling for line and a knowledge of how to make the cello

Work	Date	Composer
Konzertstück opus 12	1906	Ernst von Dohnanyi, Hungary (1877–1960)
Symphonie concertante	1909	Georges Enesco, Rumania (1881–1955)
Grand concerto	1915	Heitor Villa-Lobos, Brazil
Fantasia	1945	(1887–1959)
Concerto number 2	1955	
Schelomo	1915	Ernest Bloch, Switzerland (1880–1959)
Concerto in E minor opus 85	1919	Edward Elgar, England (1857–1934)
Concerto opus 21	1922	Kurt Atterberg, Sweden (1887–1974)
Epiphanie	1923	André Caplet, France (1878–1925)
Kammermusik number 3 opus 36/2	1925	Paul Hindemith, Germany
Concerto 1940	1940	(1894–1964)
Concerto with wind orchestra	1926	Jacques Ibert, France (1890–1962)
Rhapsodie I	1928	Béla Bartok, Hungary (1881–1945)
Concerto	1929	Arthur Honegger, France (1892–1955)
Concerto number 1	1931	Bohuslav Martinu, Czechoslovakia
Concerto number 2	1946	(1890–1959)
Concerto after a concerto by G. M. Monn	1932	Arnold Schoenberg, Austria (1874–1952)
Concerto number 1	1935	Darius Milhaud, France
Concerto number 2	1947	(1892–1974)
Suite Cisalpine	1954	
Concertino	1936	Albert Roussel, France (1869–1937)
Concerto	1936	Willem Pijper, Holland (1894–1947)
Concerto	1937	Gian Francesco Malipiero, Italy (1882–1975)
Opus 58	1938	Serge Prokofiev, USSR
Symphony—Concerto opus 125	1952	(1891–1953)
Concertino opus 132 (Posthumous work completed by Kabalevsky and Rostropovitch)	1955	
Concerto	1946	Aram Khachaturian, USSR
Concert Rhapsody	1963	(1903–1978)
Concerto opus 22	1946	Samuel Barber, USA (1910–1981)
Concerto number 1 opus 49	1949	Dmitri Kabalevsky, USSR
Concerto number 2	1964	(1904–)

Work	Date	Composer
Ode to the Westwind	1954	Hans Werner Henze, Germany (1926–)
Concerto	1957	William Walton, England (1902–1983)
Concerto number 1 opus 107	1959	Dmitri Shostakovitch, USSR
Concerto number 2	1966	(1906–1975)
Dialoghi	1960	Luigi Dallapiccola, Italy (1904–1975)
Concerto number 1	1962	André Jolivet, France
Concerto number 2	1966	(1905–1975)
The Song of Orpheus	1963	William Schuman, USA (1910–)
Melodie concertante	1964	Henri Sauguet, France (1901–)
Concerto	1964	Boris Blacher, Germany (1903–1975)
Symphony for cello and orchestra	1964	Benjamin Britten, England (1913–1976)
Concerto	1966	George Perle, USA (1915–)
Concerto	1967	Frank Martin, Switzerland (1890–1974)
Cello concert	1967	Lukas Foss, USA (1922–)
Concerto	1968	Alberto Ginastera, Argentina (1916–1983)
Concerto	1970	Witold Lutoslawski, Poland (1913–)
Tout un monde lointain	1970	Henri Dutilleux, France (1916–)
Concerto	1972	Edison Denisov, USSR (1929–)
Ritorno degli Snovidenia	1976	Luciano Berio, Italy (1925–)
Concerto	1982	Krzysztof Penderecki, Poland (1933–)

sing. I have already discussed the three sonatas of Alessandro Scarlatti (1659–1725), which also exploit the sonority of the cello.

For a long time, the six sonatas of the Venetian composer Benedetto Marcello (1686–1739) were practically the only sonatas from the baroque era performed at all. They were the best known because of an edition published in 1874 in which they were revised by Alfredo Piatti. They are rather pleasant and written in a traditional style. The

Sinfonia in F major of Pergolesi, already mentioned, is a little more interesting; some of its themes were used by Stravinsky for his *Pulcinella*. The sonatas of Nicolo Porpora (1686–1768) and Martino (dates unknown) are other interesting examples of the epoch.

With Antonio Vivaldi, we arrive at an important point of development. The first edition of his Six Sonatas opus 14 was published in Paris around 1740; and both the edition and the original manuscript are still preserved in the Bibliothèque Nationale. These works show deep research and originality. Although constructed in the "da chiesa" form (the movements are arranged on a slow-fast-slow-fast pattern), they are boldly written with a vigorous rhythm, the strength of which stands out in the handling of the form. Vivaldi makes use of a diversity of technical figurations without ever falling into a superficial virtuosity, and his expressive musicianship is particularly apparent in the slow movements. Of this opus, the third and fifth sonatas are probably the most significant. Two other Vivaldi sonatas are to be found in the archives of the Naples Conservatory and another one in the library of the Chateau Schoenborn at Wiesentheid in Bavaria.

In eighteenth-century London, there were many Italian composers who more or less monopolized the musical scene. I would like to draw attention to the fact that, strangely enough, most of them were cellists. All wrote sonatas and some were even prolific—like Joseph dall'Abaco (1710–1805) who produced thirty-four. Salvatore Lanzetti (c. 1710–1780) wrote twelve sonatas, Giacomo Cervetto wrote eighteen, Pasqualini de Marzis wrote twelve, Stefano Galeotti six, Giovanni Battista Cirri twenty, Andrea Caporale six, and Giorgio Antoniotto di Adorni (1681–1766) thirteen.

The violinist Francesco Geminiani composed six Sonatas opus 5 while living in London, but they were published in Paris in 1746. The first French sonatas saw the light in this city in 1729 and 1734 with the publication of the sonatas opus 26 and opus 50 by Joseph Bodin de Boismortier (1691–1765). These are rather easy works, historically interesting and pleasant to play. Michel Corette (1709–1795) has the distinction of having written the first method for cello in 1741, part of a large series of methods for various instruments. His Sonata opus 20 bears the wonderful title "The Delights of Solitude."

Early in the 1700s, Jean-Baptiste Barrière (1707–1747), who ranked with Berteau as an outstanding French cellist, was the first composer to have a sonata for harpsichord published. His twenty-four sonatas for cello showed obvious technical progress as well as melodic study. They also foretold the direction French cello music would take in its tendency to make a great show of virtuosity—a characteristic spurred on by the remarkable development in technique made by the French School (whose dominating force would be felt until the beginning of the following century). With the sonatas of Lepin, François Cupis (1732–1808), Louis Auguste Janson (1749–1815), a great rival of Duport, and Joseph Tilliere (c. 1730–1780), this tendency was merely reaffirmed.

Of the two Duport brothers, although the younger became the more celebrated, the works of the older Jean-Pierre drew more attention. Written in a preclassical form, his twenty-four sonatas—which are divided into four sets of six sonatas each and carry the opus number 4—fully explore the cello's possibilities throughout a range that had grown to cover almost five octaves. His use of the bow demonstrates all the effects of which the French had become masters, and his melodies, although almost sugary in their sweetness, make the instrument sing marvelously.

Jean Baptiste Bréval (1753–1823), a pupil of Cupis, played at the Concert Spirituel early in his career, joined the orchestra of l'Opera in 1781, and (according to Fetis) became a professor at the Conservatoire, where he stayed for six years, in 1796 (*see Figure 21*). In 1804, he published an interesting method for cello. His compositions include quartets and trios, as well as several concertos and thirty sonatas for cello. The virtuoso quality of these sonatas heralded the next generation. From the first in opus 12 through those of opus 28 and opus 40, to the last in opus 42, all reveal a genuine development of style and technique and a use of nuance abundant for that period. The last movement of the fourth sonata of opus 28 is a set of variations on "God Save the King."

With the works of Boccherini, the cello made its entrance into chamber music as a partner with an equal role. His wonderful quintets with two cellos, in which the first has a preponderant part, are truly delightful. He wrote 113 of them, and I would like to point out particularly Gérard Nos. 265, 266, and 275. He also turned out 91 quartets and a large number of sextets, trios, and duos—as well as other combinations. His 28 sonatas for cello with accompaniment of another cello (or eventually harpsichord) are delightful and full of diversity in the writing, while remaining rather typical of the best Italian music for that era. They are admirably written for the cello, by a composer who was himself a great virtuoso of that instrument; but incomprehensibly they have been abandoned by the cellists of today.

The place of the cello in the chamber music of Franz Joseph Haydn is important if one disregards the trios in which its role is that of an accompanist. In his Quartets opus 33 to opus 103—especially in the six of opus 50 dedicated to the king of Prussia, Frederick-William II, in 1785 and in those of opus 71, opus 76, and opus 77—the cello began to be treated on an equal basis. Unfortunately, Haydn did not compose any sonatas for the cello. Nor did Wolfgang Amadeus Mozart (1756–1791), although he wrote well for it in his piano quartets and quintets and string quartets. The first Piano Quartet, which was a new genre for the period, is of special interest, as is his Divertimento in E♭ K. 563, for violin, viola, and cello. The Quintets with two violas K. 515 and K. 593, in which the music is superb, contain beautiful cello parts. For a commission by the king of Prussia, Frederick-William II, he wrote the Quartets K. 575, K. 589, and K. 590. It is here that the cello truly has a message to give. Haydn and von Dittersdorf (1739–1799) playing violin, Mozart on the viola, and the Bohemian composer Johann Vanhall (1739–1813) on the cello often gathered to play these works at the homes of their Viennese friends.

With the chamber music of Beethoven the cello came of age. In his works—the quartets particularly—the instruments converse in an exemplary way that reaches towering musical heights. In each work, the cello is treated differently, but always in a masterly fashion. Its use is particularly interesting in his Quintet in C opus 29, in the three "Rasumovsky" Quartets opus 59, and in his last quartets, those dedicated to Prince Galitsin. The one in A minor is of special interest. The Trios opus 9, opus 70, and opus 97 (the "Archduke") are other striking examples of his skill in writing for the cello.

We are indebted to Beethoven for introducing the era of the true sonata for two instruments. Before his time, works called sonatas were really "continuo sonatas" (solo or accompanied sonatas) in which one instrument plainly dominated while the other assumed a subordinate position. But the first true dialogue between equals was born with the Sonatas opus 5, numbers 1 and 2 for cello and piano, which are dedicated to Frederick-William II and preceded the violin sonatas. He composed seven works for cello and piano (not counting the three beautiful sets of variations) which cover in a fairly large way his different periods of creativity from 1796 to 1815 and stand in contrast with the ten sonatas for violin that cover just 1798 to 1803 (except for the Sonata opus 96, which was written in 1812). Beethoven rarely had the good fortune to assist in the performances of his works, and few of his sonatas for piano or for violin were played during his lifetime. By comparison, the cello works had more luck. I have already spoken of the premiere of the opus 5 sonata, given by Duport in Berlin. Opus 69 was played by Anton Kraft, while opus 102, which Beethoven dedicated to his dear friend Marie von Erdody, was presented in Vienna in 1816 by another good friend, Joseph Lincke (1783–1837)—a member of the Schuppanzigh quartet and an intimate of the Erdody family—with Beethoven's pupil, the pianist and composer Carl Czerny (1791–1857) at the piano.

I would like to add opus 17 to the opus numbers just discussed. It appeared simultaneously in two versions—one for French horn and a more elaborate one by Beethoven himself for cello. There is also an edition of the String Trio opus 3 for cello and piano, which was published in 1807 as opus 64. All these sonatas present sizable problems of execution with our modern instruments—the difference in volume between today's concert grand piano and a cello is a little too great. Consequently, in order to minimize this difference, it is often necessary to modify the original dynamic markings in such a way that the cello will not be overpowered. This problem did not arise in Beethoven's time because the instruments of that day were more evenly balanced.

The problem of balance does not prevent these sonatas from being monuments of the literature. The first, opus 5 numbers 1 and 2, begin with a slow introduction that leads to two rapid movements, a rather unusual form. Composed in 1796, they were already published by 1797. To Beethoven's great astonishment, the double bass virtuoso Dragonetti joined him in performing the second of them in 1799. The Sonata opus 17, which is dated 1800 and published the following year, is a charming work—too rarely played, although Casals often included it on his programs.

On the subject of the opus 64, which Czerny thought of as the third sonata for cello by Beethoven and which was forgotten for a long time, here are a few interesting facts. One day during the course of my research, as I cast a wandering eye over a list of Beethoven's works, my attention was caught by "opus 64" in reference to a sonata for cello and piano. I immediately made inquiries among my musician friends, colleagues, and musicologists; but no one could give me any valid information on the subject. The most frequent response was that it must be a typographic error and surely was meant to be "opus 69." Not content with this, I began a survey and investigation in libraries on two continents ending up finally at the Beethoven Archives in Bonn, birthplace of the composer. How great was my joy to discover there a copy of the opus 64 first edition of 1807. Probably intended for Anton Kraft, and perhaps written for the same reason that Beethoven made other arrangements of his own works—to "put food on the table"—it nevertheless rounds out the list of cello sonatas in a very interesting manner.[3]

One of the most popular works in our repertoire is very likely the Sonata in A major opus 69. It appeared in seventeen editions during the first forty years of its existence. Composed in 1803 and published in 1809, it was dedicated to Baron Ignaz von Gleichenstein, an amateur cellist and brother-in-law of Therese Malfati, one of the numerous objects of Beethoven's unrequited love. The most lyrical of the seven sonatas, its expressive first theme is stated by the cello alone and immediately creates a marvelous atmosphere of tenderness and happiness.

The last two Sonatas, in C and in D opus 102, are remarkable

3. I have made an edition of it, which was published by Theodore Presser Co., Bryn Mawr, PA, 1980.

examples of the production of this composer in their novelty of form and richness of invention. The first carries the title "Freie Sonate (Free Sonata)" on the manuscript, and it fully justifies this name. Made up of two rapid movements, each preceded by a slow introduction, with a reminder of the initial motif in the last part, it has an improvisational character. The first theme seems to be a continuation of a melody that had already begun before the opening of the piece.

The last sonata attains the dignified grandeur of the last quartets, particularly in the second movement—an adagio of tremendous beauty. The first movement, which is in a rather strict sonata form, is very brilliant. The third movement is a grand fugue in four voices, three being entrusted to the piano and the fourth to the cello. For a long time it was considered almost unplayable, and it was the first work published in which the cello part was printed on the piano score above the piano part so as to enable the pianist to keep his place. This format has been the practice ever since. At one of the first performances of this sonata, a critic who was unwilling to admit that he had no understanding of the work cut off a discussion of its originality to make the statement that this improbable work was playable only by virtue of the fact that the pianist could see both parts.

Among the compositions of Beethoven's contemporaries, one can find some attractive sonatas. Joseph Wölfl (1773–1816) published one in Paris in 1805 which is charming, well-written, and musically interesting. A composer and pianist, Wölfl was a competitor of Beethoven in a piano recital held during one of those musical tournaments so popular in that age; his teachers had been Leopold Mozart, father of Wolfgang, and Michael Haydn, brother of Joseph.

The cellist, Bernhard Romberg, wrote a score of sonatas in the classic style in which, however, romanticism can be detected. As is to be expected, all are very well devised for the cello. The Sonatas opus 38 and opus 43 are the most successful, the second of opus 38, in G major, being especially commendable.

Anton Kraft also wrote six Sonatas opus 1 and 2, which are less advanced in style but rather more difficult technically.

Friend to Haydn and Beethoven, pupil of Mozart at the age of eight, disciple of Albrechtsberger and Salieri, child prodigy of the piano, theorist and prolific composer, Johann Nepomuk Hummel (1778–1837) wrote a delightful "Grande" Sonata opus 104 in 1824, which he dedicated to the grand duchess of Russia. At its premiere, given by Nicolaus Kraft in 1826, it received this eulogistic review in *The Harmonicon*: "We say without any reservation that this is not only the most authoritative and beautiful composition of Hummel but also one of the best and most brilliant works of this genre that we have heard."

The Sonata number 9 in A, D. 821 of Franz Schubert (1797–1828) was originally written for a strange instrument, the arpeggione. This curiosity was a cross between a cello and a guitar. It had six strings and frets, but it was played with a bow. It was invented in Vienna in 1823 by a friend of Schubert, Georg Staufer, who asked him to write this work. The premiere of the Sonata took place the following year, performed by Vincenz Schuster, one of the few players of the arpeggione. Promptly forgotten, the instrument was relegated to the museum; but Schubert's beautiful sonata has now become part of the repertoire for cello, for which the composer wrote no sonatas. Another of Schubert's compositions, however, is often considered the greatest work in all chamber music—the Quintet in C opus 163, with two cellos. This combination of a string quartet with a second cello, conceived by Boccherini, finds extraordinary fulfillment in this work. The sound of the two cellos, playing either in unison or in thirds, or completely independently, is always used to perfection, with exceptional lyricism and drama. The writing gives full value to the beauty of the immortal themes. The interpretation of this important work—as much for its musical content as for its size—demands meticulous rehearsal from the executants, even though it lies extremely well for all the instruments. The other works of Schubert in which the cello has a privileged position are the "Trout" Quintet opus 114 (written for the Viennese cellist Sylvester Paumgartner), the Quartets number 13 opus 29 and number 15 opus 161, and the Trios opus 99 and opus 100.

George Onslow (1783–1852), a French composer of English origin and an amateur cellist, also wrote quintets for two cellos—thirty-four in fact—at the premieres of which he, himself, played the principal cello part. Totally forgotten today, he deserves to be brought back into fashion. The Quintets opus 34 and opus 58, are particularly successful, and his three Sonatas opus 16, which are highly romantic, anticipate this era with a certain lyric quality of melody.

In the year 1825—with the advent of romanticism—the very pretty Sonata of Lisogoub that I have already mentioned appeared in Russia. In that same year, Felix Mendelssohn (1809–1847), then sixteen, composed his outstanding Octet for strings opus 20. Born into a well-to-do family of Hamburg in the year of Haydn's death, Mendelssohn made his debut as a pianist at the age of nine and began to compose the following year. At twenty, he conducted the St. Matthew Passion of Bach, an event that began the posthumous fame of that great composer, and at twenty-six, he was named director of the prestigious Gewandhaus Orchestra. In his compositions, the cello has important parts—not only in the Octet, where the second cello opens the last movement playing alone and at a furious pace, but also in the Trio opus 49, where it introduces the beautiful first theme. His Sonata in B♭ major opus 45, composed in 1839, and the Sonata in D opus 58, composed in 1842, which were intended for his brother Paul who was an excellent amateur cellist, have much perfection of form and are well adapted to the cello. The second, in D, which is very brilliant and has had more success, contains an interesting section for the cello in the adagio movement. This section is in a free recitative form which ends with the "twelve strokes of midnight" (depicted by twelve pizzicato notes on the open G string) before the last movement brings the work to a close in a virtuoso manner.

I have already spoken in an earlier section of the beautiful Sonata in G minor opus 65 by Frederic Chopin (1810–1849). Worthy of the better products of this Polish composer, its success in performance is dependent on the pianist's awareness of the power of a modern piano and on his knowledge of how to control it. In Warsaw, when I had the opportunity to hear a piano that had belonged to Chopin, I found that its action was lighter and allowed one to play more delicately. With an instrument of this type, there would be no problem in establishing a correct balance with the cello, a problem I have already touched upon in regard to the Beethoven sonatas.

Robert Schumann (1810–1856) did not write any sonatas for cello. His only original work for the instrument is "Five Pieces in Popular Form" opus 102. He nevertheless gave the cello a prominent place in his chamber music, especially in the Trio in D minor opus 63, the Quartet in A major opus 41 number 3, and the beautiful Piano Quintet opus 44—a form Schumann was the first to use. The Piano Quartet opus 47, which is dedicated to Mathieu Vielgorsky, contains a lovely solo in the slow movement. Near the end of this there is an unusual requirement: the cellist is to tune the C string down to B♭ in order to sustain the bass on the octave of the final chord.

Charles-Valentin Alkan (1813–1888), over whom a curtain of silence has fallen, was an accursed composer, author of piano works of symphonic dimensions and a child prodigy at once hated and adored. In 1857, he wrote a Sonata for cello and piano opus 47 that was not given voice until almost twenty years later, in a performance in which the composer was joined by Auguste Franchomme. This work is eminently personal and extremely varied. Certain parts of it foreshadow Brahms, Tchaikovsky, and—in places—even Fauré and Debussy. Requiring two executants with consummate technique, it repays them with rich musical material. Totally romantic, its monumentality is reminiscent of Beethoven. It is in four contrasting movements, the last being a tarantella of satanic spirit that closes the sonata in a burst of fireworks.

From the Swedish composer Franz Berwald (1796–1868) we have an interesting Duo in B♭ major opus 7, composed in 1859, which ought to have a place on the programs of concerts of today. The celebrated pianist Anton Rubinstein (1830–1894) composed two Sonatas opus 18 and opus 39, of which the latter in particular sings well and is pleasant to play.

With Johannes Brahms (1833–1897), we arrive in a world where the cello is king; he gave it a privileged place in all his chamber works. Every one is worthy of mention, but most particularly are the Trios opus 8, opus 87, and opus 101; the Clarinet Trio opus 114 and the Clarinet Quintet opus 115; the two Piano Quartets opus 25 and opus 60, and the Piano Quintet opus 34; the String Quintet opus 88; and the two Sextets opus 18 and opus 36. And of course I must not neglect Sonatas for cello and piano opus 38 and opus 99, and the recently rediscovered opus 78. The E minor Sonata opus 38, composed in 1862 at the request of Joseph Gausbacher, opens with a movement full of lyricism, goes on to a "quasi minuetto" evocative of the baroque, and ends with a three-voice fugue. The F major opus 99 was composed in 1886 and given its premiere the same year by Brahms and his friend Robert Hausmann. This superb work, full of ardor and spirit, reaches the summits of expression in its marvelous adagio, continues with a difficult scherzo (which includes a lyric trio), and ends with a rondo of bucolic character. It dates from an idyllic August Brahms spent in Switzerland on the shore of Lake Thun, the same month that saw the birth of his beautiful Violin Sonata opus 100 and the Trio opus 101.

Until a few years ago, cellists had only these two Brahms sonatas to play, but then another was miraculously unearthed. I am referring to a version for cello of his Violin Sonata number 1 in G major opus 78, the admirable "Regenlied" Sonata, based on a theme taken from the celebrated lied of the same name. It is probable that Brahms made this arrangement at the behest of Robert Hausmann, who had given the first performance of the opus 99 and for whom he wrote the Double Concerto. It was the last year of his life, and perhaps Brahms did not feel strong enough to write an entirely new work, so he took the violin sonata, transposed it into the key of D major, and made a host of minor changes—about 180. (For example, the melody at the end of the work is taken away from the piano and given to the cello.) The composition was finished in 1897, just before the composer's death and published by Simrock the same year. The edition consisted of very few copies, and it disappeared shortly thereafter. Its recovery and addition to the repertoire marvelously complete the series of Brahms cello sonatas.

It is regrettable that Peter Ilyitch Tchaikovsky (1840–1893) did not finish his sonata for cello, but he gave some beautiful moments to the instrument in his Trio opus 50, written "to the memory of a great artist" in posthumous tribute to Nicolas Rubinstein, and in his famous First Quartet opus 11, one of his works most strongly influenced by Russian folklore. The slow movement, andante cantabile, which has been arranged for a variety of instruments, is based on a peasant tune found in Kalouga. One arrangement, done by the composer himself, calls for solo cello with string orchestra.

There is a cello version of the pretty Sonatine for violin opus 100 by Anton Dvořák (1841–1901), but it is in his chamber music that this composer favored the cello. One can cite especially the Trios opus 65 and opus 90 (the "Dumky"); the Quartet opus 80, and the Piano Quartet opus 87; the Quintet opus 31, and the Quintet with double bass opus 77.

From France, there is an interesting sonata in A minor by Edouard Lalo (1823–1892). Camille Saint-Saëns (1835–1921) also gave us two Sonatas, op. 32 and 123. The latter, which is the more praiseworthy, was composed in 1905 while the composer was sojourning in Algiers, between "two excursions he made to visit with three 'gazelles,' friends of his." The celebrated Sonata in A by César Franck (1822–1890), for either violin or cello, is especially sonorous when played on the cello.

1883 saw the publication of a sonata in F major opus 6, by the young Richard Strauss (1864–1949). A brilliant work with fluent writing, perfectly suited to the cello, it was successful immediately. Although not often played, it remains one of the better works in the repertoire.

In the same year, the Norwegian Edvard Grieg (1843–1907) composed his Sonata in A minor opus 36, in honor of his brother Jon who was a cellist. Together, the brothers gave it many performances. Very popular, it was played first in Dresden by Grützmacher and later by Klengel, while Casals interpreted it an incalculable number of times on his world tours. Alas, it is unjustly ignored in our day.

With the sonata in F♯ minor opus 1, of the German composer Hans Pfitzner (1869–1949), who should be better known, and the four Sonatas opus 5, opus 28, opus 78, and opus 116 of Max Reger (1873–1916), this panorama of cello music in the nineteenth century comes to a close.

The place of the cello in the chamber music of the twentieth century is extremely important and would justify a work devoted solely to this captivating subject. It was not only among quartets (Debussy wrote the G minor quartet in 1893—the year Tchaikovsky composed the Pathétique) that a totally new path would open in this type of music. Consider the Sextet opus 4, "Verklärte Nacht," which Schoenberg wrote in 1899, and the Ravel Quartet in F of four years later, which was followed in 1908 by the debut of six quartets by Bartok. In 1909, Webern produced his Five Pieces opus 5; and in 1910 the Quartet opus 3 of Berg appeared. In 1941, while a prisoner in a Stalag, Olivier Messiaen (1908–) composed his noteworthy "Quartet for the End of Time." This series of works continues in the present with the Quartet (1976) of Henri Dutilleux (1916–), one of the more remarkable examples of recent works.

One should not forget the marvelous works for eight celli by Heitor Villa-Lobos (1887–1959), a cellist himself, Bachianas Brasileiras number 1 (1932) and number 5 (1938–45) with soprano voice.

The sonatas for cello and piano also form a very important list. From it I have included the most significant in the table on pages 154 and 155.

THE CELLO IN THE ORCHESTRA

It has been thought that because of the exceptional popularity of the viola da gamba in seventeenth-century France, the cello was introduced there relatively late; but it has now been confirmed that the instrument was already played by 1556 under the name *basse de violon* (*see Figure 11*). The first known work to make use of it dates from 1581. This was the *Ballet comique de la reine*, written by a musician from the court of Catherine de Medici, Balthazar de Beaujoyeux, to be performed at the marriage of the duke of Joyeuse (*see Figure* 9). The music includes an air, "La Clochette," composed by Lambert de

Work	Date	Composer
Sonata in G opus 19	1901	Serge Rachmaninov, Russia (1873–1943)
3 Sonatas, in F sharp minor	1902	Jean Huré, France
in F major	1906	(1877–1930)
in F sharp major	1909	
Sonata opus 8	1903	Ernst von Dohnanyi, Hungary (1877–1960)
Sonata in G minor	1904	Guy Ropartz, France
Sonata number 2	1916	(1864–1955)
Sonata opus 4	1910	Zoltán Kodály, Hungary (1882–1945)
Sonata in A major opus 20	1911	Albéric Magnard, France (1865–1914)
Sonata (one movement alone)	1914	Anton von Webern, Austria (1883–1945)
Sonata	1915	Claude Debussy, France (1862–1918)
Sonata number 1	1915	Heitor Villa-Lobos, Brazil
Sonata number 2	1916	(1887–1959)
Sonata	1917	Frederick Delius, England (1862–1934)
Sonata number 1 opus 109	1918	Gabriel Fauré, France
Sonata number 2 opus 117	1922	(1845–1924)
Sonata number 1	1919	Willem Pijper, Holland
Sonata number 2	1924	(1894–1947)
Sonata	1920	Arthur Honegger, France (1892–1955)
Sonata opus 11	1922	Paul Hindemith, Germany
Sonata	1948	(1895–1964)
Sonata opus 29	1925	Alexandre Tcherepnin, Russia
Sonata opus 30, number 1	1925	(1899–1977)
Sonata opus 30, number 2	1928	
Sonata opus 6	1932	Samuel Barber, USA (1910–1981)
Suite Italienne	1934	Igor Stravinsky, Russia (1882–1971)
Sonata opus 40	1934	Dmitri Shostakovitch, USSR (1906–1975)
Sonata number 1	1940	Bohuslav Martinu, Czechoslovakia
Sonata number 2	1941	(1890–1959)
Sonata number 3	1952	
Sonata	1948	Francis Poulenc, France (1899–1963)
Sonata	1948	Eliott Carter, USA (1908–)

◇ GREAT MOMENTS FOR THE CELLO ◇

Work	Date	Composer
Sonata opus 119	1949	Serge Prokofiev, USSR (1891–1953)
Sonatina	1949	Nikos Skalkottas, Greece (1904–1949)
Sonata opus 32	1959	Arkady Trebinsky, France (1897–1982)
Sonata opus 65	1961	Benjamin Britten, England (1913–1976)
Sonata opus 75	1962	Dmitri Kabalevsky, USSR (1904–)
Sonata	1963	Alexei Haieff, USA (1914–)
Sonata	1964	Roberto Gerhard, Spanish-English (1896–1970)
Sonata	1971	Edison Denisov, USSR (1929–)

Beaulieu and Jacques Salmon for the whole family of violins. This is the first printed work to contain a clearly designated part for the cello. Since then the cello's role has continued to grow. Its essential harmonic function, recognized by all, makes it an integral part of all symphony orchestras. Berlioz said in his *Treatise on Orchestration* of 1844, "The timbre of the cello is one of the most expressive in the orchestra. Nothing is more voluptuously melancholic, nor more appropriate to voice tender and languorous themes than a large group of cellos playing in unison."

Certain passages in celebrated works are indissolubly linked with the cello. One example is the *William Tell* Overture of Rossini with its cello solo, accompanied by four other cellos—a few unforgettable pages. "The Swan" from *Carnival of the Animals* by Saint-Saëns is another example that has gained an exaggerated popularity. I could speak of many other instances of this type in which the cello has an important place, but I would rather discuss its genuine contribution to the great masterworks of symphonic literature.

The cello is found in the majority of the works of Lully and Rameau; while in the compositions of Bach and Handel, cellos are the foundation of the entire tonal structure. Handel entrusted a few solos to it in his concertos and concerti grossi; but as was the case in chamber music, the cello made its true entrance in the symphonies of Boccherini and Haydn. In the minuet of Haydn's Ninth Symphony, there is a solo that gives the cello its full import, to say nothing of the famous passages in symphonies 31, 88, and 95. His Symphonie Concertante opus 84 for oboe, bassoon, violin, and cello gives the last instrument an interesting and difficult part that frequently requires playing in the violin range. In Mozart's operas as well as his symphonies, there are some beautiful passages such as the accompanying "obbligato" to an aria in *Don Giovanni*, and very interesting ones in *The Abduction from the Seraglio*.

In all Beethoven's orchestral music, the cello is always important—it sustains the basis of the harmonic structure and at times joins with others in the melodic line. It can be entrusted with a big virtuoso solo, as in *The Creatures of Prometheus* ballet, or auspiciously combine with the double basses to give the exposition of a fugal theme, as in the third movement of the Fifth Symphony, or state the marvelous theme—so full of joy and despair—of the finale in the Ninth Symphony.

Schubert, Mendelssohn, and Schumann always made the cello sing. In Liszt's works, it appears continually; and Wagner had a special affection for it. As for Berlioz, he always used it brilliantly. Brahms could not do without it. Even in the slow movement of his Second Piano Concerto he wrote such a lovely cello solo—with the piano taking second place—that at the conclusion of a performance of this work it is often amusing to see the pianist obliged to shake the cellist's hand and (albeit reluctantly) share the applause of the audience with him.

I could multiply these examples to infinity because the cello is absolutely indispensible in the orchestra. There are still to be considered the symphonic writings of Tchaikovsky, Dvořák, Mahler, and Strauss, as well as the works of Ravel and *La Mer* of Debussy. And then we have the operas of Rossini and, above all, of Verdi. Closer to us in time are the works of Stravinsky, Prokofiev, Shostakovitch. I have already passed over an enormous number of works, but the few names I have mentioned ought to recall to us the importance of the role the cello plays in all orchestral music.

THE UNACCOMPANIED CELLO

It is in the realm of the unaccompanied cello that the most interesting disclosures can be made because this area covers all the literature of the instrument from its very beginning up to the modern experiments of the avant-garde musicians.

I have already written about Giovanni Batista degli Antoni, Domenico Galli, and Domenico Gabrielli. In 1689, Gabrielli wrote seven ricercari with a pen full of spontaneity and a multiplicity of ideas that appear at every instant. The cello is supposed to be tuned in this way:

a tuning prevalent during that era, notably with Antonio Gianotti and G. B. Vitali. However, the ricercari can be played without any problems on a cello tuned normally. These works, the first fruits of a form of writing that has continued to develop until the present, presaged thirty years in advance the musical monument of our repertoire, the six Suites for unaccompanied cello of Johann Sebastian Bach (1685–1750). Written at Cöthen around 1720 during one of the most pleasant and productive periods in his life, they represent the suite form at its highest point of development. The beautiful melodies, the perfect counterpoint, the completely satisfying harmonies, and the lively rhythms capture the entire spirit of the dance in all its varieties.

Since the holograph manuscript of these suites has unfortunately been lost, a copy dating from Bach's later period in Leipzig, made by his second wife Anna-Magdalena, until recently was the only source of reference. For this reason, performers of these works were faced with a number of problems: her copy contains many errors in notes and measures; it lacks clarity; and it completely omits some important markings such as ornaments and clear indications for bowings, tempi, and dynamics.

After searching for a long time for the most reliable documents I could find, I had the good fortune to locate two copies in Marburg am

Lahn, Germany, made by two Bach enthusiasts which had eluded the attention of musicologists for over a century. One by Kellner, the other by Westphal; both are now in the Staatsbibliotek in Berlin.

Johann Peter Kellner (1705–1772) was an organist at Grafenrode whose copies are responsible for the preservation of several of Bach's works. We have reason to believe that his twenty-five-page copy of the cello suites dates from the same year as his copy of Bach's violin sonatas—1726.

Johann Jacob Heinrich Westphal (1756–1825) was an organist at Schwerin. His later copy of these suites, written in a large hand and covering forty-two pages, remained in the possession of the Westphal family until the nineteenth century. It was eventually acquired by the Prussian State Library.

Compared to that of Anna-Magdelena, the copies of Kellner and Westphal have fewer errors. In addition, they are more lucid in the matter of bowings and they indicate some tempi and dynamic markings. They also contain a few ornaments. By cross-checking them against Anna-Magdalena's copy, and with the version for lute of the fifth suite in the Royal Library in Brussels, which is in Bach's own hand, I was able to establish a practical edition for the execution of these suites.[4] This was published in the United States in 1964, the same year I had the pleasure of presenting it for the first time in one concert at Carnegie Hall. Since then, in my quest for a greater authenticity, I have come to the conclusion that the best way to perform these suites is to use a baroque cello with a bow of the same period (*see Figure* 17). Once the different technique is well mastered, the sound produced—because of a lesser tension, lower pitch, and gut strings—is transparent and more relaxed, yet warmer. With the old-style bow, one can obtain very articulated strokes, making the bowings of Bach's time more understandable. The result is a more vibrant performance.

All the Suites for unaccompanied cello by Bach are written on the same plan: a prelude, followed by an allemande, a courante, a sarabande, two "Galanterien," and a closing gigue. Most of these dances,

4. I must acknowledge the encouragement and moral support of the great cello teacher Luigi Silva (1903–1961) in this undertaking.

still in fashion during Bach's time, were often danced at both court festivities and country festivals. It is interesting to take note of the following descriptions of these dances and their individual characteristics taken from a work by J. Mattheson (1681 – 1764), *Der vollkommene Kapellmeister* of 1739:

Allemande: portraying a satisfied mood, enjoying order and repose.
Courante: sweet hope, full of joyous cordiality.
Sarabande: expressing no passion other than pride.
Minuet: a measured joy.
Bourrée: As its name depicts—replete, satisfied and pleasant.
Gavotte: A leaping movement is the property of the Gavotte, without having the least semblance of running.
Gigue: The common—or English—gigues have the characteristic of impetuosity and ardor. The French gigue [like that in the Fourth Suite] was not written to be danced. It is impelled by a great speed: "from something which seems unvarying at first, and which then accelerates to the flow of a small torrent."
Louré: The Louré "shows pride and has something of the bombastic about it." [The gigue in the fifth suite is rather in the style of the louré.]

The idiom most frequently used by Bach in these suites is the melodizing of harmony. Chords are used to underline and emphasize the cadences, while sustained monody without accompaniment is used only occasionally and just for contrast. The composer displays great skill in giving the impression of several voices, although the writing is on one simple melodic line.

The six Suites present a wide diversity of character and treatment:

First Suite: This is the lightest of the six, full of confidence and gaiety. The prelude is reminiscent of the first prelude in the Well-Tempered Clavier in its use of pedal point throughout. The courante is in the Italian style; the Gigue ends the work in an atmosphere of optimism and cheerfulness.

Second Suite: This suite exploits the expressive resources of the cello on the highest level. Its atmosphere, both tragic and lyrical, which can be felt from the opening of the prelude, is underlined by the use of the minor mode. The allemande is reminiscent of the second partita for unaccompanied violin, while the courante displays a desperate energy.

Third Suite: This suite is the most frequently played. Its principal emotional characteristic is one of heroic optimism. In form, it is particularly well balanced, the movements all being based on the tonic chord. The prelude is in a toccata style; and Kellner indicates at its beginning that it be played presto. There are two bourrées—the second he calls "bourrée piano."

Fourth Suite: This suite has a vigorous and robust quality. In the prelude, by the simple use of eighth notes Bach gives the impression of organ playing. This suite could have been written for a keyboard instrument. The two bourrées are authentic peasant dances; the gigue, which is in 12/8 time, calls for the fastest tempo possible.

Fifth Suite: This suite is called the "Suite Discordable" because it requires scordatura: the A string must be lowered to the pitch of G. There is a version for the lute which is very rich and elaborate, while the version for cello is the most finely detailed of all the suites. Its particular quality is one of solemn grandeur much akin to that of certain organ works. From the beginning, it is evident that the prevailing mood is one of classical tragedy. The prelude—the only one of its kind—is in the form of a French overture: a slow introduction in the style of a fantasia, followed by one of Bach's longest fugues—an amazing tour de force, more important than any of those in the Well-Tempered Clavier. The courante is typical of the French style. The sarabande, the only dance written without double stops or chords, reaches a summit of lyric beauty with a single melodic line. The gavotte II is in rondo form; and the gigue produces an almost satanic effect with its repetitions of similar motifs.

Sixth Suite: This suite is written for a five-stringed cello, the additional string being tuned to E. Inspired by the increased range this gave the instrument, Bach allowed free rein to his instinct for virtuosity. The entire suite is replete with an exuberant optimism. The Westphal manuscript gives some very detailed and carefully annotated directions for nuances in the prelude. In both the Westphal and Kellner copies the Allemande is marked molto adagio and adagio. The sarabande is an uninterrupted succession of chords that make the fullest use of the profound resources of the cello. Gavotte II is French in spirit—it is actually a musette in that it reminds one of bagpipes and hurdy-gurdies through the effect it produces by using a pedal point on the tonic. The gigue closes the suite in an atmosphere of jubilation.

The musicologist and biographer of Bach, Philipp Spitta, has said of these suites: "The decisive character of the dance-forms places them almost above the violin suites, and they show just as much inexhaustible fullness of invention." The violin suites were probably composed during the same period. It is also necessary to mention the twelve "Toccate a solo" and the sonatas written by the Neapolitan cellist Francesco Paolo Scipriani, or Supriano, (1678–1753), still unpublished, which were discovered by Luigi Silva in the library of the Conservatory of Music, San Pietro a Majella, Naples. Scipriani may have been Franciscello's teacher.

The suites are the only compositions Bach wrote for the cello. In addition to their musical importance, they demonstrate a thoroughly investigated knowledge of the instrument and a desire to exploit and enrich its resources. They are conceived in the same spirit that would later inspire Chopin in his piano etudes and Paganini in his violin caprices. Let us not forget that Bach himself was a great virtuoso, so that his feeling for virtuosity was entirely natural.

We can only conjecture about the identity of the artist for whom these works were composed: some think they were intended for Bach's friend Christian Ferdinand Abel, an eminent gamba player and excellent cellist; others suggest they were intended for Christian Bernhard Linigke of the Cöthen Orchestra.

Since the first publication of the suites at Leipzig in 1825, the inaccuracy of Anna Magdalena's copy has been the pretext for more than fifty editions, some of which even include the addition of a piano accompaniment. No less a composer than Robert Schumann perpetrated one of these, but it was never published.

Their unprecedented originality placed these suites in a category that was unique, to which no other examples would be added until almost two centuries had passed. For some unknown reason, the literature for unaccompanied cello traveled through a long black tunnel and did not emerge until 1915—a date which marks the beginning of a period extending to the present which has seen the publication of more than two hundred works in this form.

The connection with Bach was made by the Three Suites opus 131c, of the German composer Max Reger (1873–1916). These works, which are in no way imitations of his great predecessor's but evocations written in a very different style, are dedicated to three famous German cellists of that era: Klengel, Becker, and Paul Grümmer. Straddling two centuries, Reger—who was deeply attached to Brahms—was simultaneously a belated romantic and a precursor of modernism, whose chromatic expressionism presaged Schoenberg while his archaic neoclassicism anticipated Stravinsky and Hindemith. These suites, which date from 1915, are extremely well written for the instrument and should not be scorned by cellists. As representatives of an age of transition in music, they are sufficiently interesting to be used successfully on recital programs.

In the same year, the Hungarian composer Zoltán Kodály (1882–1967) wrote his monumental Sonata opus 8, the first important work in this genre to be published in the twentieth century. Since then, numerous composers have followed his example, and the repertoire for solo cello is constantly growing. Around the turn of the century, Kodály—along with Béla Bartok—was an avid discoverer of Hungarian folk music. It is estimated that these two composers managed to transcribe about four thousand melodies; and this research, with the knowledge it afforded, was bound to emerge in their use of folk-like thematic and rhythmic material in their music. One feels it especially in this work of Kodály, which introduces effects and sounds new to the era. The score requires that the two bottom strings be lowered to F♯ and B. Consequently, the notes to be played on these two "out-of-tune" strings are written a half-step higher than they actually sound. Since the prevailing key of the piece is B minor, this tuning makes it possible to play arpeggios on a constant pedal point of B. It is clear that Kodály, who was a cellist himself, wanted both to show off the cello's full potential and to compose one of the most complete works ever written for a stringed instrument. The score, which extends over a range of five octaves, demands a great deal from the executant with its many varieties of pizzicato notes in both hands and its harmonics, trills, and tremolos. At the same time, special sound effects are created by bowing very close to the bridge or over the fingerboard. However, these effects are controlled by the obvious mastery of the composer and are used solely in a musical way. This intensely lyrical work is in three movements, of which the first and last are in sonata form while the second is in three parts. The whole is constructed on a very large scale, and the playing time is about thirty minutes.

Egon Wellesz (1885–1976), a disciple of Schoenberg and a specialist in Byzantine music, published his Sonata opus 31 in 1923 and his Suite opus 39 in 1927. These two works are well written and very pleasant to play.

The Sonata opus 25 number 3 (1923) by the renowned German composer Paul Hindemith (1895–1964) is a small masterpiece. Written in a very concise manner (its duration is scarcely ten minutes), it consists of five contrasting movements typical of the composer's style at that time. They are arranged in an "arch" form, the third movement is the keystone, flanked on each side by the second and fourth which join with the outside first and fifth that form the pillars. Although this work is fascinating, it is rather easy to play.

The following year saw the publication of a Sonata for cello in C opus 28 by the celebrated Belgian violinist Eugene Ysaye (1858–1931), who had written six unaccompanied sonatas for his own instrument. Influenced by French music—Fauré especially—and by Reger, Ysaye tried to make a synthesis of these two styles in a somewhat rhapsodic form, but he was not totally successful. Occasionally, the writing is almost violinistic, but it is always playable on the cello. It is a short work comprising four pieces of different character.

During the same period, the Czech composer Alois Haba (1893–), while doing extended research on a musical system made up of intervals smaller than half-tones, published a Fantasie in Quarter-tones opus 18. In 1955, he followed with a Suite in Sixteenth-tones, which is practically impossible to play.

Well suited to the instrument, the Suite by the cellist Gaspar

Cassadó is flattering for the interpreter. Its themes, inspired by the folklore of his native Spain, give a particular lustre to the cello.

In 1931, pianist Artur Schnabel (1882–1951) composed a Sonata in honor of his friend Gregor Piatigorsky. In spite of his immense technique, this great cellist considered the work difficult and ungrateful to play, but it is possible that his judgment was colored by an incident that occurred years earlier. Schnabel and Piatigorsky gave a series of concerts in Hamburg and Berlin, together with the violinist Bronislav Hubermann and Paul Hindemith as violist. Schnabel raised the question of how the artists' fees should be distributed and made the following proposal: "As there are thirteen works to be played—three quartets, three trios, three violin sonatas, two viola sonatas, and two cello sonatas—this makes a total of thirty-five individual parts. Since the piano is involved in every work, the distribution should be 13/35 for the pianist, 9/35 for the violinist, 8/35 for the cellist, and 5/35 for the violist." His partners were speechless and resentful at this astounding arithmetic. It could be that a memory of this incident influenced Piatigorsky's evaluation of Schnabel's sonata. The work does present problems, but it deserves to have an artist master them and give it a chance to be heard. Although very close to Schoenberg in its style, it is nonetheless highly personal. The writing is at times tonal, at times atonal, or even bitonal and chromatic, but it is always well studied and redolent of care for solid construction.

The Suite opus 84 of Ernst Krenek (1900–) is the first example of serial writing in a work for unaccompanied cello. *Serial writing*, an idiom that Schoenberg developed, is also called *twelve-tone* because it uses the twelve tones of the scale in a predetermined sequence (tone row). The five movements of the Suite, all based on the same row, brilliantly demonstrate a complete and thorough use of this mode of composition. Published in 1942, this work, which does not present any great difficulties for the executant, is pleasant to hear.

In 1945, the Italian composer Luigi Dallapiccola (1904–1975) composed three remarkable pieces—Chaconne, Intermezzo, and Adagio. His writing, which is influenced less by Schoenberg himself than by his disciple Alban Berg, reveals in these pieces consummate mastery, profound musicianship, and a fervor close to mysticism.

Dalla ɔiccola was deeply stricken by the tragic political events of the war, and his concern is reflected in the way he uses the cello to express war's horrors and violence, although he ends on a note of hope for peace.

An example of serial writing in an almost baroque context can be found in the charming Serenade of the German Hans Werner Henze (1926–). This work is a succession of nine very short pieces in different styles.

In 1950, Jacques Ibert (1890–1962) wrote two pretty pieces, Etude-Caprice as a monument to Chopin and "Ghirlarzana." The first was a commission from UNESCO to celebrate the centennial of the death of Chopin. Although it seems a little strange to use an unaccompanied cello to render homage to the great Polish pianist, several of Chopin's themes are used in the composition. The other piece, which is also a tribute (to the memory of Vera Koussevitzky, wife of the orchestra conductor), was commissioned by the Koussevitzky Foundation. Its title meaning *wreath* or *garland*, this musical offering is a pleasing *pièce d'occasion*.

On the other hand, the Second Sonata of Henk Badings (1907–), published the following year, turned out very well. In some respects, it recalls the Kodály Sonata; but it always retains its own individuality. Written by one of the most serious representatives of the Dutch School, it is in three sections played without pause and is extremely well constructed and interesting throughout. It is a significant work that needs to be played with virtuosity.

During the last months of his life, Serge Prokofiev (1891–1953) worked on a Sonata for unaccompanied cello opus 133, but he was able to complete only a major part of the first movement before his death. The rough drafts he left were sufficient to make completion of the movement possible, however, and this has been done recently by a musicologist in Moscow. The work is typical of Prokofiev's style—extremely lyrical, even romantic—and it makes the cello sing in its best registers. After the exposition of the theme and its development, there is a slightly burlesque section that makes judicious use of left-hand pizzicato to create a sound of accompaniment. A brilliant climax is reached before the recapitulation of the first theme guides the movement to a calm but expressive end. One can only regret that the other movements were never written.

In 1957 in the United States, Ross Lee Finney (1906–) gave us a brilliant Chromatic Fantasy in E; and in 1959, Gunther Schuller (1925–) produced his Fantasy opus 19. At the time of these writings, Finney was a professor at the University of Michigan and Schuller, a great expert on jazz, was director of the New England Conservatory in Boston.

Ernest Bloch (1880–1959), the Swiss composer who was a long-time resident of America, wrote three Suites for unaccompanied cello. They are relatively simple in the writing, they have no insurmountable problems of execution, and they are attractive; but although they are rhapsodic in style, they never come close to the grandeur of the composer's celebrated Hebrew Rhapsody *Schelomo* for cello and orchestra.

Of the works from France, I would like to single out the charming Sonata of Henri Sauguet (1901–), dated 1956 and dedicated to me; the Concert Suite of Andre Jolivet, composed in 1965; and the *Explosante fixe* of Pierre Boulez (1925–), written in memory of Igor Stravinsky in 1973.

During the same year, Betsy Jolas (1926–) published a small piece, "Scion," which is very successful, very accessible, and an excellent introduction to contemporary music for the cello.

With the Sonata of Bernd Aloys Zimmermann (1918–1970), written in 1960, and the "Caprice for Siegfried Palm" of Krzysztof Penderecki (1933–), published in 1968, we enter a new era in which traditional musical notation is replaced by diagrams that are often very decorative and look more like sketches by Paul Klee than regular music scores. These brilliant works give an enormous amount of freedom to the instrumentalist, a fact which makes them paradoxically something of a return to the improvisational style of the Renaissance and the baroque era.

The great English composer Benjamin Britten (1913–1976) has added to our repertoire three big Suites opus 72, opus 80, and opus 87, written in 1964, 1967, and 1974, and all dedicated to Mstislav Rostropovitch. As important for their form as for their content, these works show a vast knowledge of the technique of the cello, not surprising in light of the affection of the composer for the Russian cellist. The most successful are the first and the third; the second has some interesting parts, but it makes little bid for repetition. Opus 72 has an intriguing form: its six movements—fuga, lamento, serenata, marcia, bordone, and moto perpetuo—are connected by four parts called cantos primo, secondo, terzo, and quarto. All are played without interruption. The cantos are chorales in which the cello is able to sing fully. The serenata is entirely in pizzicato. In the bordone, a D is sustained throughout the duration of the movement, giving the effect of a drone bass similar to that one associates with bagpipes or with the rustic hurdy-gurdy. Although Britten's personal style of composition is stamped with a certain neoclassicism, he does not disdain to profit from modern experimentations. In these suites, he has advantageously made the most of the great potential of the unaccompanied cello.

Iannis Xenakis (1922–), "that musician unlike the others," as he was described by Olivier Messiaen (with whom he studied after first being a pupil of Hermann Scherchen), is a man of universal interests in the manner of the scholars of the Renaissance. An avant-garde composer who did serious research on Byzantine music while he was acquiring a thorough knowledge of mathematics and a degree in architecture at the Athens Polytechnic School, Xenakis seems always to be totally engrossed in all his activities. A member of the Resistance during World War II, he came out of the war with very grave injuries to his face—a face beautiful in profile and appearance, in which sadness hides a certain malice. Around 1947, he became the faithful collaborator of the great architect Le Corbusier, with whom he worked out plans for the development of such noteworthy projects as the Convent of Ste. Marie de la Tourette, the Radiant City at Marseilles, and the Palace of the Assembly at Chandigarh, India. In 1958, Xenakis designed the revolutionary Philips Pavilion at the World's Fair in Brussels; and in 1964 he organized the music and lighting ambiance of the one in Montreal.

From 1955 on, his knowledge of mathematics led him to use this science in his composing, an activity he had been pursuing concurrently. He said of this: "It is a tool for work, a universal language, an accomplishment, a pleasure, a joy in abstract play." This is what one feels in his *Nomos Alpha* for solo cello, which he composed in 1965 for the German cellist Siegfried Palm, a great specialist in contemporary music for the instrument. The title of this admirable work means "fundamental law." It is dedicated to the memory of Aristoxene of Tarentum, Evariste Gallois, and Felix Klein. This music is symbolic and, in the words of the composer himself, "A thorough exploration of the structure of groups and of structures beyond time. This theory is of prime importance and concerns abstract objects or figures which have a certain relationship between them. For example, in arithmetic, if an addition is made of integers which are elements of a group, their sum gives another element of the same nature to the group. Zero is a neutral element as it changes nothing if you add it to an element. You have opposites which are the negatives. In geometry take the polygon: a group is born of the rotating movement of that polygon around an axis or one of its summits. With a triangle, you would have only three possibilities in the relationship of one apex to the other two and, as with the polygon, the group would be cyclical, limited, and closed in nature; whereas, with numbers the group is infinite. In music there are all kinds of things one can discover and use while confined within the rules of this internal logic."

Nomos Alpha uses a traditional notation on one, two, or three parallel staves and employs certain special signs to indicate the divisions of tones—particularly those divided into quarter-tones and those which are done for the purpose of creating an entirely new effect: that of acoustical "beats" produced by two adjoining strings ringing in sympathy.

In performance, this piece always causes a great sensation. It is a spellbinding work that presents the cello's possibilities in an absolutely new light. As Bach marked a new stage in the development of the instrument 240 years ago, Xenakis—in our time—is demonstrating with his scientific logic that the prospects for the cello are unlimited. In 1977 he wrote *Kottos*, another very interesting work for solo cello, which I played in its first Parisian performance in 1979.

I should mention also the twelve works written at the suggestion of Mstislav Rostroprovich for the seventieth birthday in 1976 of the Swiss conductor and patron of the arts, Paul Sacher. Most are based on the letters of his name:

Conrad Beck, Für Paul Sacher
Luciano Berio, Les mots sont allés
Pierre Boulez, Messages
Benjamin Britten, Tema "Sacher"
Henri Dutilleux, Hommage à Paul Sacher
Wolfgang Fortner, Thema und Variationen
Alberto Ginastera, Puneña number 2 opus 45
Cristobal Halffter, Variationen über das Thema eSACHERe
Hans Werner Henze, Capriccio per Paul Sacher
Heinz Holliger, Chaconne
Klaus Huber, Transpositio ad infinitum
Witold Lutoslawski, Sacher-Variationen

These pieces are not all of the same quality or importance, but all are welcome additions to the solo cello repertoire.

The enumerations of these works that comprise the great moments for the cello in music will serve, I hope, to aid music lovers and amateurs, professionals, concert organizers, and those who wish to build a record library, in giving the cello the place it deserves while, at the same time, they are discovering the wealth of material in this territory that is still unmined. This leads me quite naturally to the subject of the repertoire that is in greatest need of revival. It would be very interesting to restore to favor certain forgotten or misjudged composers. For example, I would like to mention Romberg, his concertos (which are successes in the classic style) and some of his sonatas. There is also B. Molique, whose Concerto opus 45 Hans von Bülow said was "the best concerto written for cello, . . . with a first movement recalling the Violin Concerto of Mendelssohn, . . . but more original." This work is a specimen of what could be incorporated into our concert programs. I mention only less celebrated composers because we have already seen how much of the work of Vivaldi, Boccherini, Haydn, and others still remains unknown. Why is the Second Concerto of Saint-Saëns never played? Why is the "Epiphany" of André Caplet, which is a true masterwork, consistently ignored?

Accordingly, a great deal remains to be done; and I am applying myself to doing it with all my soul.

Postlude

A GREAT DEAL of what you have read in this work is the fruit of my experience as a concert artist and as a musician curious about everything that concerns the instrument I love. To discover, study, and interpret works for the cello is my life, and I would like it very much if all of you could share with me the joy of understanding more fully all that a cello "is." I am well aware that I have merely skimmed the surface of this subject; but I hope I have given you a desire for further knowledge and—of greatest importance—the wish to become better acquainted with the music for the cello. If you have learned only one new thing from reading this book and, what's more, if you have found the text entertaining, then I have attained the goal I set for myself.

Bibliography

If you wish to examine our interesting subject more thoroughly, here is a selection of books, taken from a long list of several hundreds I consulted in compiling this work. Unfortunately, there are very few books devoted solely to the cello.

Bach, Johann Sebastian. *Six Suites for Cello Solo.* Edited by Dimitry Markevitch. Bryn Mawr, Pa.: Theodore Presser Company, 1964.

Baillot, Levasseur, Catel et Baudiot. *Méthode de violoncelle adoptée par le Conservatoire Impérial de Musique.* Paris, 1805. Geneva: Minkoff Reprints, 1974.

Baines, Anthony. *Musical Instruments through the Ages.* Harmondsworth, Middlesex: Penguin Books, 1966.

Blees, Gisela. *Das Cello-Konzert um 1800.* Regensburg: Gustav Bosse Verlag, 1973.

Boyden, David. *The Hill Collection of Musical Instruments.* Oxford: At the University Press, 1964.

———. *History of Violin Playing from Its Origins to 1761.* Oxford: At the University Press, 1965.

Casals, Pablo. *Joys and Sorrows: Reflections as told to Albert F. Kahn.* New York: Simon & Schuster, 1970.

Cobbett's Cyclopedic Survey of Chamber Music. Second ed. Oxford: At the University Press, 1963.

Corrette, Michel. *Méthode théorique et pratique pour apprendre en peu de temps le violoncelle dans sa perfection*. Paris, 1741. Geneva: Minkoff Reprints, 1972.

Cowling, Elizabeth. *The Cello*. New York: Charles Scribner's Sons, 1975.

Donington, Robert. *The Interpretation of Early Music*. London: Faber and Faber, 1963.

Doring, Ernest D. *How Many Strads?* Chicago: William Lewis, 1945.

Eisenberg, Maurice. *Cello Playing of Today*. London: The Strad, 1957.

Gerard, Yves. *Thematic, Bibliographical, and Critical Catalogue of the Works of Luigi Boccherini*. Oxford: At the University Press, 1969.

Goodkind, Herbert K. *Violin Iconography of Antonio Stradivari, 1644–1737*. Larchmont, N.Y.: By the author, 1972.

Guinzbourg, Lev. *Istoriya Violontchelnovo Iskusstva*. 4 vols. Moscow: Muzika, 1950, 1957, 1965, and 1978.

Hill, W. Henry. *Antonio Stradivari: His Life and Work (1644–1737)* London, 1902. Reprint, New York: Dover Publications Inc., 1963.

Hutchings, A.J.B. *The Baroque Concerto*. London: Faber and Faber, 1961.

———. *Mozart, the Man, the Musician*. BAARN Phonogram Int., 1976.

Itzkoff, Seymour. *W. Emanuel Feuermann, Virtuoso*. University: University of Alabama Press, 1979.

Jalovec, Karel. *Italian Violin Makers*. London: Paul Hamlyn, 1958.

Kinney, Gordon James. "The Musical Literature for Unaccompanied Violoncello." 3 vols. Ann Arbor: University Microfilms Inc., 1962.

Lutzen, Ludolf. *Die Violoncell-Transkriptionen Friedrich Grützmachers*. Regensburg: Gustav Bosse Verlag, 1974.

Marx, Klaus. *Die Entwicklung des Violoncells und seiner Spieltechnik bis J. L. Duport (1520–1820)* Diss. Regensburg: Gustav Bosse, 1963.

Mersenne, Marin. *Harmonie Universelle*. Paris, 1636. Reprint, Paris, 1965.

Milliot, Sylvette. "Le violoncelle en France au XVIIIeme siècle." 2 vols. Diss. Lille, 1981.

The New Grove Dictionary of Music and Musicians. Edited by Stanley Sadie. London: Macmillan Publishers, 1980.

Newman, William S. *The Sonata in the Baroque Era*. Chapel Hill: The University of North Carolina Press, 1959.

———. *The Sonata in the Classic Era*. Chapel Hill: The University of North Carolina Press, 1963.

———. *The Sonata since Beethoven*. Chapel Hill: The University of North Carolina Press, 1969.

Panum, Hortense. *The Stringed Instruments of the Middle Ages*. London: Reeves, 1939. Reprint New York: Da Capo Press, 1975.

Piatigorsky, Gregor. *Cellist*. New York: Doubleday and Co., Inc., 1965.

Pincherle, Marc. *Les instruments du quatuor.* Paris: Presses Universitaires de France, Collection Que sais-je?, 1948.

Poidras, Henri. *Dictionnaire des luthiers.* Rouen: Imprimerie de la Vicomté, 1924.

Quantz, Johann Joachim. *Versuch einer Answeisung die Flöte traversiere zu spielen.* Berlin 1752. Modern English translation by E. R. Reilly. London: Faber and Faber, 1966.

Riley, Maurice W. "The Teaching of Bowed Instruments from 1511 to 1756." Diss. Ann Arbor: University Microfilms Inc., 1954.

Rothschild, Germaine de. *Luigi Boccherini, sa vie, son oeuvre.* Paris: Plon, 1962.

Sandys, William, and Forster, Simon A. *The History of the Violin.* London: William Reeves, 1864.

Schäfer, H. "Bernhard Romberg, Ein Beitrag zur Geschichte des Violoncells." Diss. Bonn, 1931.

Shaw, Gertrude J. "The Violoncello Sonata Literature in France during the 18th century." Diss. Ann Arbor: University Microfilms Inc. 1963.

Silverman, William Alexander. *The Violin Hunter.* New York: The John Day Co., 1957.

Straeten, Edmun S. J. van der. *History of the Violoncello, the Viola da Gamba.* London: William Reeves, 1915.

Vatielli, Francesco. *Primordi dell' arte del violoncello.* Bologna: Pizzi C., 1918.

Index

NOTE: *Italics* denote appearance in an illustration.

F

G

H

W

X

Y

Z

Alfred